BLESSED
— *by* —
DEATH

**A GRIEF JOURNEY FROM PAIN
AND SADNESS TO PEACE AND SACREDNESS**

Alena Kupchella Gourley

Book Design by
Transcendent Publishing

Editing by Dana Micheli

Author photography and headshot by Courtney Claypoole of 84 Photography
Makeup by Madi Toy

ISBN: 979-8-9906867-9-3

Disclaimer: This book does not provide medical advice. The book is for informational purposes only and provides my personal experiences. No material included is intended to be a substitute for professional medical advice, diagnosis or treatment and never disregard professional medical advice or delay in seeking it because of something you have read in this book. Call or text 988 for the Suicide and Crisis Lifeline.

Printed in the United States of America.

For my husband Matt – your belief in me and your unending support allowed this book to happen. And for my children – Issadora, Jacob, Ian, and Bodhi. I love you to the moon and back.

TABLE OF CONTENTS

"No one gets out of this world alive, so the time to live, learn, care, share, celebrate, and love is now."

~ Leo Buscaglia

"Life will give you whatever experience is most helpful for the evolution of your consciousness. How do you know this is the experience you need? Because this is the experience you are having at the moment."

~ Ekhart Tolle

PART 1:

Introduction

HOW DEATH HAS SHAPED ME

This book is for you if you feel called to expand your understanding of the Universe, energy, religion, spiritual beliefs, and death, both physical and the death of self. It's for you if you want to explore your own grief and what it has meant in your life. It's for you if you want to find greater peace and live with more sacredness and intention. It's for you if you want to improve your connection to your loved ones in Spirit. Or, maybe, you aren't sure what that all means but feel called to explore your understanding of All That Is. This is my journey of expansion and growth via the deaths I have experienced and the death of self that happened along the way.

I am the mother of a dead child. I am a sister to a dead brother. I was with my uncle and my cousin as they took their last breaths. As I sat in school, my grandma died. As I worked in a pub in England my on-again-off-again college boyfriend died. I was with each of my animals at their end.

I think when most people think of death it's in a negative light. For me, each experience with death allowed me to grow in beautiful and necessary ways. This doesn't mean there isn't heartache and longing. There were – and are – tears, anger, and wishing the death hadn't happened and, with it, the loss of my expectations for the future. But because I am a spiritual being having a human experience, I know that this is what I'm here for – to experience the love and loss, the joy and sadness, the anger and forgiveness, the wanting for things to be different and accepting things as they are, the stuffing of emotions and feeling all the feelings. All are part of my human journey.

I grew up in a very small town in Western Pennsylvania, one of five children from my parents, two of whom have died. I went to Catholic school from kindergarten to twelfth grade. I had a grandma who prayed the novenas AND talked about her near-death experiences. She talked about her "knowing" when she and my grandpa went to San Francisco for the first time that it wasn't *really* her first time. Later, you'll read more on how her near-death experiences and waking past-life experience led to my current work.

I have forty-five first cousins and seventy-eight second cousins; the family tree branches out from there. I spent every Sunday at both sets of grandparents' houses playing with cousins. I always felt "big feelings" – whether my own or someone else's, an empath long before I knew the name for it. The Oxford Dictionary defines this as a person with "a paranormal ability to feel or know the mental or emotional state of another." It has also come to be understood as a trauma response, when one needs to assess another's mood to remain safe, physically, mentally, and emotionally. I can feel other people's pain and emotions. If you have ever walked into a room where no one is talking but you can sense there was just a fight, it's similar to that.

No one knew how to help me with those big emotions; it was more about keeping a stiff upper lip and exploiting any weaknesses. I think this came from the very difficult immigrant experience of my grandparents and great-grandparents, who passed down that survival-of-the-fittest-by-any-means-necessary attitude. Everyone was welcome, but you better be able to hold your own! I was lucky enough to know two of my great-grandmas and all four of my grandparents, and I learned from their strength and resiliency.

Looking back, I can see now that my "imaginary friends" weren't really imaginary. They were my Aunt Theresa, who had died young, and my sister, who died before she had a chance to be born. I recently came across a clip of me at four talking about them and it hit me that I was experiencing them from the other side.

My driving force and passion is to help people feel and function at their very best. But it's equally important to me that we walk that path together. You are the expert of your life; I am the expert in optimizing the mind to support you in living the life you want, free from physical mental, emotional, or spiritual pain – and working to heal whatever needs healing so that can happen.

It started with my wanting to be a physician – either a heart transplant surgeon, able to turn a death into a blessing, or a forensic pathologist, solving the mysteries surrounding deaths. In high school I started a community service program. In college I spent my spring breaks repairing homes in Kentucky; later, after bailing on medical school, I volunteered for a whole year in the same program. I then went into social work with a mental health concentration and served in many different arenas, including relatively brief stints in a juvenile sex offender facility as a wrap-around case manager and therapist; at a domestic violence shelter, teaching doctors' offices how to spot child abuse; and in a nursing home as a case manager. Longer opportunities followed: one-on-one therapy, medical social work in the hospital, and on an inpatient geriatric psychiatric unit. Later, I opened my own business, beginning with past-life work then birth education, essential oils, and nutrition products. Then I realized with my past life and full hypnosis certifications I could make that my business focus. I am passionate about brain and holistic health – mindset really is everything!! It is about harnessing the power of the mind and integrating our spiritual side with the practical application of day-to-day life.

A lifelong learner, I am always studying disciplines and subjects I feel called to and incorporating them into my work with clients. I also regularly draw on the lessons from my personal experiences. My individual sessions are customized based on the greatest need of the client's soul. Some people come to a session saying that they don't know what they need, they just know they want things to be different. I am good at distilling down the presenting problem, and as we talk we always move into an understanding of what to work on. Once we enter hypnosis, the soul and subconscious will take us exactly where it most needs to go for the greatest healing.

We work on alleviating any physical, mental, or emotional pain, exploring current or past lives as needed. This helps to gain clarity and insight. It allows the client to do for themselves what they most need to do – be it forgiveness of others or self; saying what they didn't get a chance to say at the time; soul-to-soul communication with those alive or deceased; and, most importantly, taking care of themselves in the ways they most needed but didn't get. Sometimes a soul hug of your younger self makes all the difference.

I also do everything from energy work with chakra clearing and balancing to intergenerational healing and inner child work, addressing past trauma, anxiety, depression, addictions, and so much more. In addition, I offer group classes, combining what I'm learning on my own spiritual journey with what I study professionally and from other spiritual leaders. These groups are either scheduled by me or someone who brings together a group of friends or family or as a guest at retreats. A goal of mine has been to offer retreats. I was set to offer one in 2023 with Alexandra Wyman, but I postponed it to donate a kidney to my dad. The when, where, and with whom is still to be determined for a future retreat. After traveling to sacred sites in Glastonbury, Avebury and London, it would be a dream to bring others there on retreat to experience the divine healing it offered.

Group hypnosis is something I mostly do around seasonal changes; it helps with that energy shift and engages the participants in a conscious conversation with me and their Spirit Team. We identify what they need and want to let go of in the practical sense or beliefs that no longer serve them. Then we identify what they want to bring into their lives, how they truly want to be living. I weave that together for a beautiful group hypnosis that incorporates their intentions with the current energetic and astrological shifts.

"Death is a stripping away of all that is not you. The secret of life is to 'die before you die' and find that there is no death."

~Ekhart Tolle

I have a very personal reason for doing what I do: I have been to the depths of not wanting to be here anymore. Some might think I'm being dramatic; to others, it makes perfect sense. And because I can be a dramatic bitch, or that big feeler I mentioned earlier, I thought it meant actual, real-deal death. What I've come to realize is that in those times I wanted to physically die, what I really needed was the death of old paradigms – the end of a narrow view of the world and of myself so I could open to possibilities and opportunities all around.

This is indeed a type of death, what I call a "death of self," and it is the shedding of old layers of oneself, just like a snake sheds its skin. To talk about death of self feels tantamount to helping others be seen and feel understood. I am sharing my story, but I have witnessed and heard the same experience from many of my clients. In turn, they, along with my training, have helped me further understand my own experiences.

The Toltec teachings Don Miguel writes about in *The Four Agreements* refer to a process of domestication. In this process, Miguel writes, "… you learn that you need to be a certain way in order to be accepted, and because it's not okay to be what you are, you start pretending to be what you are not. You form an image of what it means to be perfect, but you can never measure up to that ideal."[1]

Human Design, another area that I have studied to help me in understanding myself, my family, and my clients, talks about conditioning.

---

[1] Miguel, Don. (1997) *The Four Agreements: A Practical Guide to Personal Freedom (A Toltec Wisdom Book)*. Amber-Allen Publishing, Incorporated.

Parkyn writes, "…along the way, we've picked up and collected traits and acceptable responses that are deemed the 'norm,' so there's always a tendency to act as we believe we should act, or how we've been trained to act, all the time keeping our inner beings bound and gagged."[2]

The death of self happens when we recognize what no longer serves us.

As I started writing this book, I worried a lot about what others might think of me – especially those who are a part of my life and may have a different perspective about an event or experience. As we go through life, our brains and souls latch onto particular beliefs or stories, to the point that we accept them as absolute truth. I do believe we come to Earth with a plan of how our soul will grow and expand, including the lessons (showing up as experiences) that assist that growth. For some, it seems to always be one thing after another, while others have long periods of ease between lessons. But, ultimately, your soul is here to experience exactly what it is meant to and then we decide how we move forward from that.

I have been through a death of these old stories and beliefs about myself, the world, and my place in it. I have done so much work to fully forgive and completely love and accept myself. What has become clear to me, however, is that death of self will be an ongoing journey. I learned this when our son Bodhi died during labor on December 6, 2021.

In this book, I unabashedly explore my life experiences, and the beliefs I once held, unfiltered for my healing. This isn't about blame or finger-pointing – quite the opposite. I actually have a deep belief in the importance of personal responsibility, and sharing is my way of taking full responsibility for my beliefs, feelings, and actions moving forward. I can't heal unless I can be brutally honest about what I felt, what I experienced, the things that happened with other people, and the choices I made. That said, when I *do* heal, others around me heal

---

[2] Chetan Parkyn Human Design: Discover The Person You Were Born to Be

as well, and that helps heal the collective consciousness. Your healing does the same.

This is about radical self-acceptance and radical self-love and radical self-forgiveness. Simply that. Because as I work through those aspects, I learn how to help others be their best selves. Owning my story allows me to be the creator of my life and be in control of my thoughts, feelings, and behaviors. Always learning, growing, and expanding allows me to understand my shadows, honor the boundaries I need for peace and well-being, and continue striving to improve the world.

Others have their own experience and their own perception – maybe even of the same event – and that's okay. It happens all the time. We are always filtering the world through our lenses, our life experiences, and our perspectives. And that's how it's meant to be.

I was blessed with a deep well of empathy and have always been curious about other people's experiences. I credit that to reading a lot and traveling, even at a young age. This allowed me to broaden my horizons, expand my viewpoints, and realize that I'm not always right. People who thought they were always right made me uncomfortable, and it was something I never wanted to emulate. But often the shadow parts we most try to push away will rear their ugly heads; thus, I've spent parts of my life being a know-it-all, thinking I knew best, thinking what I thought was the right thought.

The more I experience of life, the more I realize that this is so far from the truth. My Catholic faith was important to me, but I couldn't wrap my head around the idea that it was right and every other religion was wrong. I'm not arguing against having your beliefs – absolutely have your own beliefs and your own moral compass! It's vital for our well-being. In my belief system, however, it can't be at the cost of others. It can't be to judge others. It can't be to think you're better than others.

The more I've connected to the other side and my Spirit Team, the more I realize that we are all on our own paths. And the more past life regressions I've done, the more I realized that we must honor our own experiences and struggles for what they are. We can't diminish our experience because someone else has it worse or better. They have their path and I have mine.

I started doing this when our baby died. I felt so lucky and blessed that we had an amazing support system, that we were treated so well by the nursing staff in the hospital, by the funeral home, that so many people were so generous, and that I had an excellent surgeon who was able to repair my fourth-degree tear without lasting effects; it goes on and on.

However, that does not take away from the fact that our baby died and that I had massive physical fallout from that birth – or that I have to live with this as my final birth experience.

I hear it all the time: people either "one-upping" – saying their experience is the worst thing that has ever happened to anyone, ever – or diminishing their own pain and struggles because other people have it worse. And, yes, absolutely keep it in perspective. Offer gratitude for your beautiful journey and the beautiful blessings in your life, but not at the expense of diminishing what you are going through. Your path is exactly what it's meant to be for the growth of your soul in this life.

I see this every time I witness a past life regression. Whatever they experienced in that life was to help them expand and grow in a certain way, just as my experiences in this life are helping me expand and grow in the way that is perfect for my soul's journey.

"Every Birth brings its Death with it; no one can escape from it."

~Ehsan Sehgal

Another aspect I'll be sharing is Death Through Birth. Through the birth of each of my children, layers of old stories and beliefs about myself and the world fell away. Each was another shedding, another death-of-self moment, an awakening, a shift into my actual, true self. These are not comfortable processes; however, as I have learned for myself and tell my clients, it is worth it. As with the actual deaths I experienced, I had to learn how to change the narrative of grief from self-punishment and recrimination and discover the blessings.

In this process, I came to understand that I didn't need to lose myself to grief, that I could actually thrive because of what I've experienced. I also utilized certain practices and activities, which you will read about, that were incredibly helpful in alchemizing my grief, allowing me to shift and change, grow and elevate my life, and love and accept myself exactly as I am in the moment. This was occurring in the midst of all the emotions −sadness, anger, guilt, regret, shame, and more. It's not a pushing away of those things, but acknowledging them, processing them, and understanding them on an even deeper level.

I'll be starting with Bodhi's story because this is where I am today. This is the me that has navigated many tragic deaths throughout my lifetime, the times that I wanted to die, and the me that can now look back in contemplation to find the blessings and lessons in each step of my life. First, though, I have included some explanations about the beliefs and experiences that guide my life and work.

My greatest hope is that you read with an open mind so you can find the ways to embrace your grief and find the ways you've been blessed by death.

AN EXPLANATION ON SOUL CONTRACTS

I believe, and have witnessed in sessions, that we make soul contracts before we get here. These are made to learn the lessons that allow our soul's growth and expansion. This doesn't make the difficult lessons any easier, but it does help me look for ways to grow and expand, to find the blessings and how to use them to help others.

I once did a past life session for myself and went to a life where my current husband was my husband and we had two children that died. But in that life, we turned away from each other and the community; we withdrew into ourselves and withered away. That regression was several years ago, yet I have found myself calling on those memories to remember to take care of myself and our family and to come together in the aftermath of Bodhi's death. Indeed, in this life we all came together with the plan of navigating child loss and recognizing the opportunity to do things in a different way. This was a monumental life lesson among many other lessons and purposes to pursue in this lifetime.

Gaining clarity and insight into the past life has helped me identify the lesson more readily in this one.

Meeting and marrying my husband was a shifting point. It tuned me back into understanding that we can recognize each other on a soul level, that there are many paths but one destination. In fact, after meeting him, I could see that there would have been other paths to doing so if I hadn't acted on the first opportunity. He balances me out perfectly, even though we can butt heads since we are both stubborn. We are both loyal and would do anything for those we care about. He is steadfast in himself and is not worried about what others think. He has a love for the land and outdoors that inspires me to get out in all weather. He reminds me that I am smart and beautiful and capable, as often as I need it. And I remind him to be silly and laugh more, to be gentler and softer. We have been through many ups and downs, but always come out stronger. He is the perfect partner for me and the best father for our kids.

He and I work so well together that I often joke it has taken us many lifetimes to get it right.

Our past lives (or, if we let go of time and space as we know it, "parallel" lives) serve as a road map of our soul's journey, and exploring them helps us navigate this difficult human experience in so many ways. It can bring a much greater sense of peace with our path. It can also allow us to experience the in-between times when we return to the God energy surrounded by unconditional love and peace.

AN EXPLANATION OF HYPNOSIS

Hypnosis is a deeper state of relaxation that allows our brain-waves to shift into a state where we can access our subconscious memories and beliefs. It's a way to access a place we can go to feel really good and let all tension and pain melt away. A place where we can make any change we wish and heal past hurts.

The Cleveland Clinic defines hypnotherapy as "a heightened state of concentration and focused attention." Guided by a certified hypnotist or hypnotherapist, hypnosis allows you to be more open to suggestions for making healthful changes in your perceptions, sensations, emotions, memories, thoughts, or behaviors.

My clients and I use hypnosis in many different ways. We use it to access current life hurts, heal past traumas, and shift into living the life we most want.

We can use it to access past lives, galactic, or interdimensional lives.

The other sessions include Hypnotic Healing and Connection to the Body. We ask ourselves, *What are my physical, mental, emotional or spiritual needs? What is my body trying to tell me? What thoughts, feelings or emotions have I tucked into places?*

We work together to answer those questions.

We open communication with the body to access the messages it is offering through physical, mental, or emotional pain.

We work together to address the hurt and pain through guided meditation and practical applications.

Several thought leaders have explained the mind-body connection and the way the body stores past hurts and traumas. To explore this more in depth I suggest *The Body Keeps the Score* by Bessel van der Kolk, M.D.; *The Secret Language of the Body* by Inna Segal; and *You Can Heal Your Life* by Louise Hay.

The other way I utilize hypnosis is in Transforming Grief sessions.

The grief can be around the death of a person or animal; it can also involve the loss of expected life outcomes. We walk through the grief journey together to heal traumas around the death and find greater peace. We bring forward the happy special memories for greater understanding and ease. We work toward gaining a greater clarity and understanding of life path and loss of expectations. We work to let go of what holds someone back from harnessing their intuition, thus, allowing a greater connection to the energy of a loved one on the other side. It is a welcoming in of the connection in a new way, and being able to see the signs, symbols, and synchronicities they are using to communicate.

We are energy, and energy is never destroyed; it only changes.

Hypnosis is also used to access and understand intergenerational trauma and gain the gifts from our ancestors; understand the chakras and balance them; access the between times when we are with Source; visit the Akashic records; prepare for labor and birth; attain space and energy clearing, and so much more. Whatever reason it is used, it can truly change any thought, behavior pattern, and physical, mental, emotional, or spiritual pain. It can also simply allow us to spend time in complete relaxation, peace, and love.

And, as mentioned, it can be used to access a past life, which I'll explain next.

AN EXPLANATION
OF PAST LIFE REGRESSION

In 2008, I traveled to Angel Valley in Sedona, Arizona to learn about, and obtain a certification in, past life regression. At that time I had been a practicing therapist for two years and was already feeling called to take the tools I offered to a deeper level of understanding and potential healing. What I learned is that we carry certain things – mentally, spiritually, and even physically – from one life to another.

Cells are the building blocks of the body – blood, organs, tissues, everything. Cell memory is the storing of trauma – emotional, physical, or mental – in those cells. It can be a bad breakup, grief, abuse, neglect, anything that impacts you over a period of time. You can also carry the traumas or old stories and beliefs of your parents, grandparents, and other ancestors.

The scientific community has acknowledged this link – and it is called epigenetics. The Centers for Disease Control defines epigenetics as, "the study of how your behaviors and environment can cause changes that affect the way your genes work. Unlike genetic changes, epigenetic changes are reversible and do not change your DNA sequence, but they can change how your body reads a DNA sequence."[3]

---

[3] https://www.cdc.gov/genomics/disease/epigenetics.htm

What's more, our cells and our subconscious minds store information from *all* our previous lives. When I journey with people to the memories they hold in their cells, I often hear something like the following: "I have always felt nostalgic, peaceful, and almost obsessed with waterfalls and flowers in this life. When I journeyed back with the intention of finding out why, I found that a favorite view from my castle, one I could rarely pull myself away from, was of a waterfall and wildflowers."

Of course, there can be painful places to explore within our cell memory as well. People have past life regressions for many reasons. They might have unexplained physical pain, like a sharp pain in their back, only to find during their past life journey that an actual spear in their back injured or even killed them. Other times, the pain is from their current life and stems from a betrayal or other emotion that got stored in the body.

They might have an unexplained fear or phobia. One of mine was being trapped in small places – not like an elevator, but more so being trapped underneath something. I can even have a very visceral, anxiety-filled reaction if I'm reaching underneath the bed and suddenly feel like I've gone too far and am going to get stuck. When I went back to look at where that fear came from, I found a past life in Egypt. I was working to build the pyramids and one of the stones fell on me. It was behind a wall that was already built and nobody found me. That was how I died in that lifetime.

Some people come to me because of a preoccupation with death – be it anxiety around death, visions of death, or other things related to dying. Oftentimes this is because their last death or a traumatic death is still lingering within them – for example, many of my clients had lives during the Holocaust. It can also be that there was some kind of unfinished business at the time of their death. Whatever the circumstances, we go in and heal all that we need to around that death so they can find that place of peace again.

I've noticed a fear of death in our culture. It's talked about in hushed tones and dealt with in hospitals or nursing homes or hospices. Now, that is necessary when it comes to medical care that can't be provided in the home; however, it often comes about because families don't live intergenerationally anymore. They also don't have time to care for the elderly or sick or dying.

One thing I have learned over the many years of walking people through their past lives is that the death is usually the least interesting part. This, despite the fact that we've accessed murders or otherwise tragic or unexpected deaths.

I bring that to you as an opportunity for a perspective shift – that of viewing death as just something that happens, even when the circumstances seem "newsworthy." This shift not only helps release fear around death; it can also inspire you to take action in your life or maybe even advocate for change in laws or policies.

My belief is that we need to be preparing for death from the moment life starts, living as if tomorrow isn't promised. This is not meant in a morbid way, but in an expansive, give-zero-fucks, limitless, impacting those around you for the highest and greatest good, offering your soul gifts to the world, living your best life kind of way.

The practicalities of a past life regression session are as follows. We start with a nice relaxation. I usually include a chakra balancing, which helps clear out any stuck energy (yours or others) and brings every-thing into alignment. Then we set the intention. You may not be sure what intention you'd set, but I'm very good at helping people home in on what they most need at that time. Or, we leave it open to the soul, always trusting that it will take us exactly where you need to go for the greatest healing and growth at this time.

Once we set the intention, we begin the process of walking backward in time until we choose the life that our soul most needs to explore. There is almost always a parallel with your current life, providing an opportunity to heal something that needs healing and gain clarity about the purpose or lesson in what you are experiencing.

After walking through the practical aspects of that life – where you lived, your family, how you spent your time – we go to three important events that most likely have a parallel with your current life. Then we move into the death of the body in that lifetime. As we move toward the light, toward Source, we are surrounded by the wisdom of the Ascended Masters, as well as our guides, ancestors, angels, the nature elementals, and our animal friends. The most beautiful and transformative piece is returning to that space of unconditional love and complete understanding.

As we do your life review, we look at the purpose, the lesson, how your soul evolved, how your soul could have done better, and if there are any people from that lifetime that you know in your current life. Sometimes there are even animals from your past life that come back in your current life. Then we look at the messages. What would your past self like to tell you? What would you like to tell your past self?

Next is forgiveness, which is a truly sacred and transformative aspect. Relationships are complicated but show up to teach us exactly what we need to learn. They might last a short time or a lifetime. Sometimes they show us how we want to be; other times, how not to be.

We ask if there is anyone who needs to forgive you and if there is anyone you need to forgive. Remember that forgiveness is for us and for our souls. It never excuses or condones behavior. The forgiveness work I offer in sessions has nothing to do with any religious affiliation.

The most important question is, "What do I need to forgive in myself?" My belief is that self-forgiveness is at the heart of all healing. This can include everything from forgiveness for our day-to-day mess-ups to forgiveness around a death, especially a tragic one.

Finally, we integrate all you learned and experienced, carrying forward the insights and clarity, the lessons learned, and the messages that will be the most helpful and healing to your soul.

PART II

The Death of Our Son, Bodhi Grant

CHAPTER 1

MY LIFE IS NOW DEFINED BY BEFORE BODHI'S DEATH AND AFTER BODHI'S DEATH

A s we neared forty, Matt was moved to part-time; he was looking for a new line of work and was back at home after six years of living and working on the road. We had spent the last year reconnecting, spending time in nature, hiking every week, finding amazing waterfalls and gorgeous rocks, and really allowing Mother Earth to help us heal the many trials and tribulations we had faced when he was working away.

We decided to try for a fourth baby, just as we had consciously decided to call our previous pregnancies into our lives. We weren't sure of the outcome because we'd had a very early miscarriage in 2019, but we were hopeful. The miscarriage was over my birthday while we were on a vacation, and though it was sad the lake and birch trees that surrounded us soothed my soul.

Sure enough, in April 2020 we found out that we were expecting a December baby.

We were thrilled. Sure, it felt a little crazy with our ages, but a little fun as well.

We did a fun *Friends* theme announcement. We planned another homebirth and decided not to find out what gender we were having. I went into the pregnancy in the best shape of my life but had a lot of major hip pain and anxiety. Looking back, I think I knew on a soul level that once the baby arrived, they would be leaving.

It was a beautiful synchronicity that Matt was able to be home for my pregnancy with Bodhi, because that's all we ended up having with him. That time he was in my belly was it. Matt got to see the pregnancy progress; he got to see and feel the belly growing and the kicks, especially because Bodhi was a mover and groover! I felt him so early, maybe even as early as ten weeks. It became evident from the outside very early as well, and for that I'm so grateful! After his birth and death there was only stillness, so I cherish the memory of that movement.

In the last few months of the pregnancy, we had significant water damage to both sides of our house that destroyed the walls in our bedroom, living room, bathroom, kitchen, and basement. The damage happened in August and no construction company was available for the repair work until October. We decided to move things into one bedroom for me and Matt so we had at least one space that was not a complete disaster. Every other room in the house was destroyed in some way or holding items from destroyed rooms.

At times it felt like a comedy of errors. We ordered tile and when it came every single piece was broken. Every. Single. Piece. My conversation with a customer service rep, a young man by the sound of his voice, went something like this:

Me, in a complete panic: "Hi, we have a really big problem with our order. I'm thirty-five weeks pregnant and planning a homebirth. We are desperately trying to get our house finished because I've had babies at thirty-four and thirty-five weeks and my house is a complete disaster, dirty every day, and I am on my hands and knees cleaning the mess from the workers at the end of each day, I can't take much more."

Rep: "I'm so sorry to hear that, ma'am. How many pieces are broken?"

Me, more calmly because I'm now numb to the absurdity of it all: "Every single piece, in all *thirty* boxes."

Rep, after a brief hold: "Ma'am, I'm so sorry. And also, I just googled thirty-five weeks pregnant and I would be a monster, a literal monster right now."

This made me laugh so hard, even in the midst of so much chaos and so much filth and so much frustration. The guys would work during the day, and then Matt would work on things at night. We had friends who came and helped us scrape wallpaper. It was an all-hands-on-deck experience.

We finished up and got things back as best we could; we gave up on finishing the dining room and kitchen wallpaper and repainting. Here we are three years later, and have yet to get back to it. Admittedly, even before the damage I was a ball of anxiety, worrying about the baby coming early and having to spend time in the NICU. After the house got destroyed, I worried the baby would come early *and* the house wouldn't be ready *and* I wouldn't have all the business things in place that I need to have in place, and on and on. A death of self around "worrying" was a shift Bodhi's death would allow.

We settled into our mostly redone space, knowing that with my pregnancy history, the baby could come any time. By the forty-week mark, however, this one was still holding on – and flipping in and out of breech position. To help with this, I was going to the chiropractor once or twice a week. That Friday, she did her magic, and later that day my midwife confirmed that the baby was head down. It was close to go time, and I was thrilled.

On Saturday I was told a family secret that rocked my world. Suddenly, I was down a rabbit hole of emotional turmoil, questioning everything I'd ever believed to be true about myself, my place in the world, and the people around me. I would love to share more because I feel every life event is an opportunity for growth and learning; however, this family secret affects others as well as me and I must respect their privacy.

The next day, our cat, Zia, got sick. She was feral, and when we got her she basically disappeared into the attic. She would come out to eat and go to the bathroom and was very leery of us, but we still loved her. A few days earlier, I was shocked when I woke to find her curled up on the bed with me. I now believe she left first to guide Bodhi back to Source.

When she got sick, she was so sick I could actually touch her and pick her up. I told her I would take her to the vet in the morning. When we woke on Monday to my water breaking, Matt went to check on Zia and found her dead. Any thoughts of not telling the kid before school quickly became moot, as they asked about her as soon as they got up. They cried many tears before they left, and would cry many more later on. We did *not* tell them about my water breaking because we didn't want them to say anything to their friends or teachers. Matt and I felt it was important to keep the news very insulated and just between us for now. Later, I'd be so scared to tell them about Bodhi's death, given their devastation about a cat that didn't even like us.

They were no sooner out the door when my labor started, fast and furious. We called the midwife and the birth photographer right away because I honestly thought I might have the baby before they got there. Instead, the labor – and excruciating pain – dragged on and on. I had delivered three babies unmedicated; I'd even been in labor with Pitocin (a synthetic hormone that brings on contractions) and no pain meds. It was hard, yes; intense, yes, but nothing like this.

I now believe the pain came from holding on so tightly, that my soul knew once he came, he'd be gone.

There is a belief that when the mother goes through an emotional experience or upheaval the baby flips head-up to be closer to her heart. Sometimes I still wonder if Bodhi flipped to breech because I'd had such an emotional upheaval that weekend.

One birth photographer had to leave and so a second one came. We still hadn't caught our family up because we just kept thinking, *Oh, the baby's gonna be here.* And it was so intense I couldn't focus or think of anything except each contraction.

I remember Issadora coming home from school and stepping over me because I had only made it to the doorway out of the tub, my pillow stained with blood and meconium. No wonder she flew past us; she is not one for the messier parts of life.

When we finally got to the point of complete overwhelm and exhaustion, I had Matt call the hospital to see which doctor would be there. We also decided to call an ambulance because I can't even tell you the level of pain I was in. The midwife encouraged Matt to help me get down the stairs because I wouldn't want to be carried down on a stretcher. As it was, I screamed with every step and, at the bottom, things became blurry. I do remember an ambulance being in front of the house. I do remember male and female ambulance staff and one of the React volunteers driving and Matt going up front. I was lying on my side. I remember before going down the stairs that the midwife had checked the heart rate and everything was strong and good. It was just supposed to be a transfer for maternal exhaustion. The only distress detected during labor was my level of pain and the incredible strength it was taking to try to push him out. If you aren't familiar with in-home midwifery care, it is very autonomous, with the mom trusting her body and the labor and birthing process. The midwife and assistant handle all medical care, emotional and physical support to the level requested by the family. They monitor the baby's heart rate and the mother's blood pressure and other vitals very closely without interrupting the flow of labor hormones.

I remember flying through town; it felt like the ambulance was going so fast. But it was all a blur. I was seeing, but not seeing, I was moving, but not moving, I was hearing, but not hearing. I had been in an internal world fighting to bring my baby earthside, even though in past labors I was in a place of allowing, this felt like an internal battle and almost all of my attention was turned inward. I now wonder if it was the ultimate connection and battle on the soul level that we needed for the birth and death to be completed.

From what I know of timelines, it was about four minutes from our house to the hospital. I remember the doctor and the nurses meeting us as we came through the emergency doors and the doctor telling me that since the baby was already coming out breech, he would perform an episiotomy. Even with the episiotomy I had to push really, really hard to get him out and needed the help of the nurses and Matt's support.

When he came out, the doctor grabbed him, and I said, "Put him on my chest, put him on my chest," and he said no. At first, I didn't understand why. And then the emergency team stepped in. They began working on him. There was a staff member by the door holding a clipboard and they would yell out everything that they were doing: "A shot of epinephrine, compressions, air!" They would count off the numbers and he would mark it down.

I was in this state of in between. I was hyperaware and yet detached. There was so much going on in the room at that point. The doctor was waiting for the placenta to come out, and it did – very quickly. There were two nurses around me, plus Matt and the doctor, the entire emergency team, and other staff coming in and out the entire time. The obstetrics doctor was focused on me and started numbing to start the stitching. Later I'd find out that I had a fourth-degree tear. And, looking back at the timeline, I was stitched for almost all of the forty-five minutes they worked on Bodhi. I remember the harsh lights, the pinching from the stitching. And the confusion, yet clarity. I kept looking at Matt and asking, "What's happening? What's happening? Is this really happening? O my God, what is happening, why isn't he breathing?"

They came over at thirty minutes and asked us what we wanted to do.

"Please," I said, knowing there was no hope but unable to give up. "Just keep trying. Please."

They worked for another fifteen minutes and came over again and said they were calling it, meaning Bodhi would be pronounced dead. However, since he never took a breath, he was officially considered stillborn. It didn't matter. All we knew was that it was over, and our life after Bodhi's death has just begun.

The room got really quiet. There was no more frantic activity. I remember the nurse wrapping Bodhi, putting the hat on him, and telling me that if I needed to scream, I could scream. But I just laid there, quietly holding him tight with Matt by my side. He looked so perfect and even had a little bit of red hair. I felt a wash of so many different things, a deep sadness, a fear of how our other kids were going to respond, what life was going to be like now that the very worst had happened. But, most of all, I just held him tight and cried many tears.

Yet, in some ways, I shifted right into practical thoughts. Who did we need to call? How did he die? How long could I have him? Do we call a funeral home? Do we plan a service? How much was the ambulance going to cost?

I told Matt that we needed to call our families. I also called the midwife, who was on her way to another birth.

"Wait, what?" she stammered in disbelief, "No, no. You were just transferring for exhaustion. What do you mean?" The other utter shock and devastation in her voice was overwhelming.

We hadn't decided on a name and, as mentioned, we hadn't even found out the sex. A name had come to my mind a few weeks earlier, but Matt wouldn't commit to it. As I laid there holding him and Matt held us both, he looked at me and asked what name I wanted. The only name that had excited me throughout the pregnancy was Bodhi, meaning "awakened" or "enlightened" in Sanskrit (बोधि). It's a Buddhist concept referring to Buddha and his followers' awareness and understanding of the nature of the Universe, and the specific spiritual awakening attained by such knowledge. Bodhi's middle name, Grant, was his paternal great-grandfather's middle name.

Bodhi was also Patrick Swayze's character's name in *Point Break*, one of my favorite '90s movies. Later, this little tidbit would bring some levity to an awful situation. When you tell someone that your baby died it can suck the energy out of a room. A special name all around.

They took me to a room and got me food. The labor had been so intense I would only get a bite of banana or grape and a sip of water before the next contraction, so I was really hungry. Back to reality. Every muscle hurt and my bottom was really, really uncomfortable. The thought of going to the bathroom was terrifying.

One of the most vivid memories I hold dear is that, as I ate, Matt held Bodhi and did that instinctive parent "rocking bounce," just as he had done with our other children. It must be something in our inherent wisdom to move in that way when holding a newborn.

It was not only the death of Bodhi, but the traumas upon trauma leading up to, during and after it, that took a toll. The difficult and excruciating labor at home. Making the decision to call to the hospital to see what doctor was going to be there and available. I don't like hospitals and I don't like doctors. Even making that call to abandon the homebirth sits in my soul with guilt and doubts – I wondered if my husband, my midwife, and the birth photographers would think I was weak and a failure if I went. Then there was the decision to call the ambulance; I couldn't just be driven there. The trauma of being dragged down the steps in excruciating pain. Sending Matt home to tell and be with the other kids. Having to put my dead baby back in the plastic crib every time I needed to get up, and almost passing out every time I had to go to the bathroom.

It didn't stop there, not by a longshot.

Being wheeled out to the hearse and handing my baby over to the funeral director. Planning a memorial service. Hand-expressing and pumping just enough breastmilk to take the edge off, but not too much to create more milk. Trying to prevent clogged ducts because you don't have a baby that would use the milk. Having guilt that you wouldn't be donating milk, yet knowing that with all the other physical issues it wasn't possible. Writing an obituary for a baby you thought you were going to bring home. Worrying how you're going to pay for an ambulance ride and a hospital stay that you weren't planning on. Putting cabbage leaves in your bra and drinking peppermint tea while you had to hug your friends and family and mourn your baby. Watching his great-grandma hold, rock and sing to him, knowing she was wishing it was her instead of him.

Having such extensive perineal stitching that you couldn't even do gentle stretching or walk too many stairs for twelve weeks – even longer for your body to regain its strength. Explaining life and death to your children, with the youngest crying that he didn't want to die because he didn't remember what heaven was like, because he'd miss us. The list could go on.

There's a grief we don't always talk about or even acknowledge: the loss of what we thought things would be. The death of Bodhi snowballed into so many aspects. Not having a new baby. No new baby snuggles, not having a new hiking buddy to put in the baby carrier, not having a first birthday, no first Christmas and fifth birthdays and preschool and all those things that we'd already outgrown with the others.

Your grief could also be about the loss of a child and the dashed expectations associated with that, or it could be for the loss of a close family, as it was when your grandparents were alive and everybody got together for meals and parties. Maybe there's a falling out and you're no longer close with someone you held dear. Maybe the spouse you thought you'd be with 'til death do you part suddenly announced they want a divorce, or you thought a particular job or a degree would lead to certain things that never materialized.

There are so many ways life throws us curveballs. That is where the struggle can live, in trying to do our best and feeling like we are failing. Feeling that we are doing everything right and it's still not good enough. At the same time, we may trust that everything works out as it should and is meant to; we might believe that we are the creators of our lives, managing our mindsets as life unfolds. Everything that happens has a purpose, and we can find and create meaning in all that occurs. We come here to learn lessons to allow our souls to expand and grow. I used to think things were happening to me; now my belief is that everything is happening FOR me – a slight shift that allows me to see the blessing and lesson in all I experience.

Understanding and integrating these beliefs has been my only way of growth through the struggle and the pain.

I could have stayed in these traumas. And it is okay for me, and for you, if you've had a devastating loss, to acknowledge all these pain points.

But this is not where I wanted to stay, so how did I navigate through and then beyond it?

It is hard to even describe the emotions we felt when we lost Bodhi. The closest I come is that it was like a near-death experience – he died within me, and a part of me died that day too.

And yet, I understand Bodhi brought me spiritual enlightenment. The experience, as awful as it was – and is – has moved me into an even greater flow with my purpose and journey for this lifetime. I was reminded to be present and stay present, especially with my family. I have acknowledged and grown in seeing the signs, symbols, and synchronicities that our loved ones are always trying to show us, but now they are unmistakable and cannot be explained in any other way. It has been truly beautiful.

The outpouring of love and support from our families, friends, our community, the kids' schools, the nurses and hospital staff, our birth team, long-lost friends, and complete strangers has been the balm for my bruised soul.

CHAPTER 2

THE LESSONS AND BLESSINGS AND DEATH OF SELF FROM BODHI

P lease read with an open mind regarding the blessings and lessons I've witnessed in my painful times so that you may see what your painful times have to offer you.

Retelling of a Taoist Parable

Once upon a time there was a Chinese farmer whose horse ran away. That evening, all his neighbors came around to commiserate. They said, "We are so sorry to hear your horse has run away. This is most unfortunate." The farmer said, "Maybe." The next day the horse came back, bringing seven wild horses with it, and in the evening everybody came back and said, "Oh, isn't that lucky. What a great turn of events. You now have eight horses!" The farmer again said, "Maybe."

The following day his son tried to break one of the horses, and while riding it, he was thrown and broke his leg. The neighbors then said, "Oh dear, that's too bad," and the farmer responded, "Maybe." The next day the conscription officers came around to conscript people into the army, and they rejected his son because he had a broken leg. Again, all the neighbors came around and said, "Isn't that great!" Again, he said, "Maybe."

The whole process of nature is an integrated process of immense complexity, and it's really impossible to tell whether anything that happens in it is good or bad — because you never know what will be the consequence of the misfortune; or, you never know what will be the consequences of good fortune.

We don't always know why things happen in the moment, but what I found over time is that after each event, each tragedy, each death, I was able to look back and see the lessons and the growth it allowed. Now, in the moment hard things are happening, I can evaluate that. As devastated as I was, and still am, about Bodhi's death, I am able to immediately begin to reframe and reassess. I am able to see those small blessings, those small gifts, and see what it was I needed to learn, where else I can let go of old beliefs and old patterns so that I can keep stepping into my gifts. Keep stepping into what I'm here to accomplish and how to help others along the way.

The thing about death is there can be so many images or snapshots that stick with us. Oftentimes they are the traumatic ones and I definitely have some of those. But I have made a massive effort to give them the space and feeling they need and then shift from those memories to the good and positive ones.

I have said to Matt that I think we're doing okay, but that's not what I meant. We definitely aren't okay; the death of a child changes you in ways that words can't really express.

But we are trying to laugh more, have more fun, connect more with our kids. It changed us in ways that have allowed us to embrace our lives fully, to let go of what doesn't matter, and to take better care of ourselves than we ever have, inviting friends over, counting our blessings and looking for ways to be a blessing to others, acknowledging the hard parts, feeling our feelings, looking for signs and symbols and synchronicities, evaluating what is really important, being close to our kids, being a family, taking risks in my business, letting go of anything and everything that has held me back.

There were many Death of Self beliefs that stemmed from Bodhi's death. It feels as if his death was the final falling away that had started within each of the deaths I had experienced earlier in my life.

I experienced a death of doubting my connection to my Spirit Team and seeing the signs, symbols, and synchronicities all around, a death of not accepting help, and a death of holding myself back from utilizing what was needed to alchemize and heal myself – mind, body, heart, and soul.

With the death of a child, it is all hands on deck; or, in this case, all healing modalities on deck. I will outline what I've used, along with some exercises for you to find what you most need in the midst of your grief.

The death of doubting my connection to the other side and those signs, symbols, and synchronicities our Spirit Team sends was a massive shift. My understanding of our Spirit Team includes loved ones in Spirit, Ancestors, Guides, Angels, animal friends, elementals, and Ascended Masters.

Of the loved ones who have died before us, not all will become part of our Spirit Team. And the Ancestors may be so far back in the family line that we didn't know them. All will have jobs on the other side and their own soul healing to do as well.

The Guides are usually beings with whom we've had past lives but stayed in Spirit while we incarnated this time around.

The Angels are beings that vibrate at a higher frequency and have never had a human life. My experience has been that we have a main angel, many helper angels, and then the Archangels.

The phrase "animal friends" was part of a prayer we said growing up. "God bless my mom and dad, my brothers and sisters, all my aunts, uncles, cousins and animal friends." I'll write much more about animals in the final chapter. For now, I will say that we can have pets that come for a reason and become Guides, we have animals that show up with symbolism and messages, and animals that are a main animal and guiding force.

I experience the elementals as an energy or being that is associated with each element. And, as an entity or being as a part of nature, like with moss or rocks or trees.

The Ascended Masters are classic religious figures, but in my experience they are an energy, an essence of certain qualities we can strive to cultivate. These beings include Jesus, Buddha, Mother Mary, Mary Magdalene, Quan Yin, and so many more whose names aren't as common.

There have been signs, symbols, and synchronicities since Bodhi that allowed that final questioning to fall away. One of my favorite signs from Bodhi happened when Matt and I traveled to the Great Smoky Mountains on his sixth-month birthday.

We hiked to Arch Rock, Inspiration Point Cave, and ended at Mt. LeConte and Cliff Top at 6,522 feet. The trail was incredibly beautiful but very challenging, and we were pretty sure that many we passed were reevaluating friendships with those who'd talked them into hiking it.

The view from the top was so gorgeous, and we took some time to honor Bodhi by reading the poem "Look for Me in the Rainbows," spreading some ashes, and honoring others we knew who had lost a baby too.

Look for me in the Rainbows

"Time for me to go now, I won't say goodbye;

Look for me in rainbows, way up in the sky.

In the morning sunrise when all the world is new,

Just look for me and love me, as you know I loved you.

Time for me to leave you, I won't say goodbye;

Look for me in rainbows, high up in the sky.

In the evening sunset, when all the world is through,

Just look for me and love me, and I'll be close to you.

It won't be forever, the day will come and then

My loving arms will hold you, when we meet again.

Time for us to part now, we won't say goodbye;

Look for me in rainbows, shining in the sky.

Every waking moment, and all your whole life through

Just look for me and love me, as you know I loved you.

Just wish me to be near you,

And I'll be there with you."

~Conn Bernard
Famously performed by Vicki Brown

On our way up we'd stopped to take many, many, pictures because it was view after breathtaking view. It was the same with all our hikes, with Matt saying in his newscaster's voice, "Five hours later..." because I just can't get enough of Mother Nature's beauty. One of the stops was at Arch Rock. When we got back to the room, I was looking through the tons of pictures and found a perfect rainbow from there.

No reason that there should have been a rainbow! There was water, but it was very low and not causing mist.

The rainbow at Arch Rock on the climb to Mt. Leconte in the Smoky Mountains.

There were so many "helpers" for us in the wake of Bodhi's death. And I finally allowed the death of not accepting help.

"When I was a boy and I would see scary things in the news, my mother would say to me, 'Look for the helpers. You will always find people who are helping.'"

~ Fred Rogers

I am going to share many of our helpers below.

A friend is a local photographer, and as soon as she found out she offered to come take pictures in the hospital. Then she came to the funeral home where we had the kids, his grandparents, and great-grandma see him before he was cremated. She even came to the memorial service. These are photos we will cherish forever.

My sister-in-law called immediately upon finding out and suggested she could come later or have my sister come right away. I would have never asked for that, but it was a true blessing having my sister there. Matt could go home to be with the other kids. She could put Bodhi into the bassinet when I needed to get up and help me to the bathroom. When she came, she brought the quilt my friend Cori had given me at my fortieth birthday party for the baby. She and her family had traveled up from Kentucky for it. It meant so much to wrap him in a quilt made with love from a long-time friend.

Alicia, a nurse at our local hospital, was not supposed to work the night Bodhi died, but she "just happened" to get called in. I put those words in quotes because I don't believe it just happened; I no longer believe in coincidence. I believe that everything and everyone we meet has a purpose of some kind. You see, Alicia had lost her own baby at three months; she knew what I was going through. When she came to see me, she asked to hold Bodhi, and she so tenderly rocked him. She has checked on me many times since and has been a wonderful support.

Susan, our nurse, has extended so much love and grace while we were in the hospital and beyond. She still tears up when she sees me.

I called upon my friends in the spiritual community – psychics, mediums, reiki practitioners, energy healers, and others. During my pregnancy I had told several powerful women and one male mentor that I would welcome their love and energetic support during the labor, birth, and postpartum period. When Bodhi died, I asked for that support even more. I know that it helped me in profound ways.

All through the night of his birth and death, I held Bodhi tucked in beside me as I fitfully slept. The nursing staff and Alex, the funeral home director, told me I could have as long as I needed. It was early the following evening when I was discharged, so Matt wheeled me to the hearse and Alex put Bodhi on the front seat wrapped in a blanket. He answered all my calls at insane hours as things popped into my mind and helped us through all the choices and in writing the obituary. He even called around and found a cradle for us to view Bodhi in before his cremation. I have a beautiful memory of Matt's grandma singing to him and holding him.

I contacted my friend, Lisa, an inter-spiritual minister, about conducting the memorial service. We talked briefly, and then she and Cindi, a mutual friend, wrote the most perfect service I could have hoped for, but never wanted. I wrote and delivered a eulogy and we had a beautiful candle lighting. She offered a guided meditation to connect with Bodhi or a loved one, which inspired the meditation you'll find below.

During the service my friend Lisa talked about dragonflies. In native and other cultures, the dragonfly is believed to be a messenger from our deceased loved ones, the angels, or fairies, and is a symbol of change, transformation, and self-realization.[4] It teaches us to love life, rejoice, and have faith even amidst difficulties. A perfect symbol at this time in our lives. When I was thirty-five weeks pregnant, I'd asked my mom to make me a minky blanket – a heavier-weight blanket that has that soothing effect. My only specification was that it be the color purple, and she and my dad decided on a purple dragonfly fabric. The dragonfly has come up many times since! And now I have a beautiful tattoo that incorporates a lighthouse, dragonfly, and rainbow, the whelk shell my uncle sent me in the Outer Banks, and my brother's signature from his suicide note, amidst dark clouds and lightning.

The wonderful thing about the signs, symbols, and synchronicities is that they are ongoing. The dragonfly showed up again shortly after Bodhi's death. It was very hard for me to go places at that time because most everyone we came across would know what had happened. I anticipated the conversation and what that was going to sound like. I would try to acknowledge Bodhi without sucking the air out of the room. I would look for the "right" words to make everyone feel comfortable, only to feel the bottom drop out of their emotions anyway. It was just too much.

I absolutely do want to talk about my son. We had very little time with him; actually, in some ways, no time with him. And yet we had so many hopes and dreams for what was to be.

So often it feels like almost he doesn't exist. Maybe he was just meant to live on in my heart. I do believe that he impacted others in ways we may never fully know. I *know* that our journey through this loss has impacted others – and that sharing it in this book will impact even more.

One of the first places we did go was to our friend Matt's birthday party. Ann and Matt are the same friends who came and helped us

---

[4] https://www.lovetoknow.com/life/grief-loss/symbolic-dragonfly-meanings-related-death

scrape wallpaper, clean, and paint. When we got there I noticed right away that my friend's mom, Debora, was wearing a dragonfly shirt. She is a sweet lady and so I knew it'd be okay to bring it up and to talk with her about it. She acknowledged that she usually didn't wear t-shirts and, for "whatever" reason, felt called to wear the shirt that day.

I have a hard time asking for and accepting help, but this allowed me to receive kindness and love in so many different forms. Longtime friends Phyllis and Shelly came to the viewing and asked me to tell them all about Bodhi and to show them all the pictures – that meant so much. I've found that most people don't know what to say and that's okay! Words fall short in these situations, but the acknowledgment is what matters. I promise, you aren't reminding the person or making things worse; it's always on their mind.

Liana and Sydney, two friends I met in doula training and had sessions with later on, wrote a poem to place on the picture of the night sky the day Bodhi died.

WE ARE ALL MADE OF STARSHINE AND CLAY

BABY BODHI GRANT GOURLEY

YOU AWAKENED & ENLIGHTENED US ALL

YOU TOOK THE EIGHTFOLD PATH

MAY YOU KNOW NIRVĀNA

YOU ARE EVERYTHING

LOVE ABOUND

ABUNDANT

The kids' school had a book made with Bodhi's name in it, which they donated to the school library. Each class sent gifts and cards and said lots of prayers for us.

Several friends brought special mementos, care packages, and art; they sat with me while I lay in bed recovering.

Complete strangers from a Facebook running group bought many Christmas gifts for our other kids.

We received so many cards and messages.

There was so much generosity in gift cards and donations, which allowed us to have time together and pay for the unexpected expenses. We received so many kind words and prayers, even from people we barely knew or had never met at all.

Matt's friend Ryan reached out right away. If anyone could understand our grief, it was Ryan, as he and his wife Katrina had lost one of their twins shortly after birth. They channeled that pain into founding Grady's Decision, an amazing foundation to help NICU babies. Ryan had also been the first person to meet our other son Jacob because he "just happened" (again with those synchronicities!) to be visiting the Dubois NICU that day. Now, after Bodhi's death, he prayed with us and talked to Matt separately for a long time.

Dads need support too!!

The death of control and worrying has been a massive shift for me.

Bodhi's death marked the end of the illusion that I have any semblance of control. At first, saying I don't have control over anything sounded and felt scary, but it is actually liberating. I can do everything "right" and things can still happen, so why waste my time worrying and anticipating the worst? I've moved into reaching for every wish, hope, and dream I can conceive of. I've come to believe that it's all about taking care of yourself, loving yourself, accepting yourself, *and* taking inspired action toward the person you want to be and the life you want to live, all while navigating the craziness of this earthly plane.

I'll share a story that highlights the struggle of letting go of these old beliefs. About two weeks after Bodhi died, we celebrated Christmas with my side of the family; we always do it before the actual day. I was good at holding it together during events, only to have a complete emotional meltdown afterward. It was a cold, Western PA December night, and as we drove home, I had my face pressed to the cold glass of the window, staring out at the stars, and sobbing.

"I know I chose this," I said silently, "I know he chose this, but I don't want it anymore." Over and over. "I know that I signed up for this, but I can't do it!"

Grief is a wild ride and it has often felt like I was out of control, but some of those "out of control" times have led to big releases. I have poured myself into my business, but there has also been a fear of missing out or the worry I'll look back with regret. I was looking forward to parenting Bodhi from this newfound place of peace I had cultivated over the last few years. I recognized I had spent too much time worrying or getting stressed and overwhelmed about things that didn't truly matter. I was holding onto guilt and shame from my past parenting choices. While I want to do big things and help as many people as possible within my business, I still want to be a present parent.

I recall one day driving the hour to my office in Indiana to deal with some fiasco. I always joke that entrepreneurship is not for the faint of heart! I can't even remember what it was now – probably a mix-up or a scheduling issue or something along those lines – but I had to let it all out on the drive home. I screamed and slammed my fist and palm into the steering wheel, over and over again. This is called somatic release and is so vital to our well-being. Any trauma or emotions that we don't process will get stored in the body.

While I will talk about movement and exercise as ways to cope with and move through grief, it can also go too far in the other direction where it becomes a way to numb or distract. After Bodhi's death, I was definitely doing too much numbing and distracting in certain areas, and my body forced me to pay attention. I have had body and food issues throughout my life – mostly binging, using food to stuff down emotions, and being very critical of my body.

In that postpartum period, with a destroyed body and no baby to show for it, plus the emotional turmoil I was in, and the increased stress of financial issues, I turned all of that inward. I thought I had healed all I needed to in this area, but as the old stories surfaced, I realized there was more work to do. I was having heart rate issues and then eventually chest pain, which was scary enough to get me to the ER and start the investigation into what was going on.

A local doctor ordered extensive blood work and heart monitoring. We discovered that I had a Lymes infection. I started Western Medicine treatment while I waited for an appointment with a chiropractor, Dr. Gallagher, for the nutrition response testing. She determined that I also had a secondary Bartonella infection. I started on a supplement protocol and reevaluated my food, finding that when I got back to avoiding all flours, all sugar and sweeteners, and alcohol, the symptoms started improving. I received further assistance in dialing in my diet and exercise from Vanessa at the jiu-jitsu gym. Such kindness and dedication to their passions allowed them to help me and so many others.

The death of holding myself back from whatever it took to heal, to process grief, trauma, and past hurts, led to seeking connection, fun, and adventure.

There are actions we take that later play out in the exact moments we most need them – sometimes years later. In 2020, I started attending Spirit Speaks online and then I joined Sunny Dawn Johnston's business group. I had met Sunny, a world-renowned psychic medium and angel communicator, and her soul musician, Kris Voelker, years earlier at an angel class in New York. You'll read about that synchronicity later in the chapter on Death Through Birth. Sunny's guidance, and the guidance of others in the group, have allowed me to step into seeing and growing my business in new and exciting ways.

Sunny called me right away after Bodhi died and talked with me and Matt. The conversation helped us understand Bodhi's purpose in not joining us earthside.

The year after Bodhi's death I was in major self-care mode. Along with a few other trips I decided to go on Sunny's retreat in Cancun. I started inner work on the flight by reading and completing the shadow work exercises in Debbie Ford's *Dark Side of the Light Chasers: Reclaiming Your Power, Creativity, Brilliance, and Dreams*. Nothing like twelve hours of reading and journaling about the darkest parts of yourself to kick off time in gorgeous Mexico! I was thankful I'd splurged and had a pool right outside my room, which I immediately sank into and cried all the tears I needed to before joining the group. They wouldn't be the last tears that week. When I joined Sunny, her amazing team, and an incredible group of women and two men, I learned that "coincidentally" there were several other women who had lost sons. Their sons were older, but we could understand each other and help each other to heal our hearts.

I swam with the dolphins, which had been a dream for a long time, and there were many beautiful synchronicities. Even the tour guide's name was Angel! The heart healing the retreat provided has kept me going; it has kept me inspired to continue to expand my understanding of Bodhi's life and death.

You will find some of Kris's music, Sunny's meditations, and some other meditations – my very favorites – in the book bonus playlist.

Swimming with the dolphins.

As part of my radical self-care that year, I called my cousin and said we needed to "crew" our Uncle Bobby for the "Javelina Jundred," a one-hundred-mile running race in Fountain Hills, Arizona. (Crewing means filling water bottles, getting changes of clothes, handing out nutrients, and even running some miles with him.) At seventy-five, Uncle Bobby was still living life to the fullest, inspiring me to do the same and have adventures while I can. We all had a blast supporting him throughout his thirty hours of racing, and I even got to be his pacer for the final twenty-mile loop. We timed out at thirty hours, making it ninety-five miles. It was quite the adventure, and I'd never been so happy to traipse through rattlesnake, scorpion, and tarantula territory to make it to the rescue truck.

Me and Uncle Bobby starting loop 5 and mile 80 at sunrise.

While there I decided I needed some time in Sedona and my parents said they would meet me there. I spent a whole day with Joseph White Wolf, a shaman, and every aspect of it healed my heart – from the

Earth connection as we navigated the wind tunnels, coffees in hand, to the secret crystal field and the hanging of the wind prayer for Bodhi. Joseph embodies a life of connecting to nature and embracing signs, symbols, and synchronicities. He inspired me to go even deeper in my own journey.

Joseph and I with our coffees

Connecting with nature at Turtle Rock

While in Sedona I was listening to Taylor Swift's new album. I had never listened to her before, but there were a few songs that resonated at this time, especially "Bigger Than the Whole Sky." There is a line where she asks if by not praying she had caused some outside force to take the person she'd lost. Hearing it was like a punch to the gut.

The song shined a light on my belief that I had done something wrong and prevented Bodhi from staying. Had I not prayed enough? Was I not good enough? In Sedona there is a Catholic church built into and on top of a hillside. I got up before sunrise and, after listening to that song and several others that allowed tears and emotions to flow, I climbed Cathedral Rock with a headlamp and headed out on a hike that ended at the church. I felt very comforted as I joined others who were praying their own prayers and fighting their own battles. I've always prayed and spiritual exploration is the forefront of my life. I have found comfort in returning to mass as my kids attend as part of their Catholic school education. The symbolism, mysticism, and the comfort provided by Jesus, Mother Mary, and Mary Magdalene have helped during this time. As I said in the beginning, I don't believe there is any right or wrong in a spiritual and religious journey; there is only what works for you as long as it is loving, supportive, and not harmful to others.

Climbing Cathedral Rock in the dark

The joy and peace of reaching the top and having the mountain to myself

Hiking, listening, praying and crying in Sedona

When I returned home, I talked to Matt about the fears that I was at fault or wasn't good enough for Bodhi to stay. He said he'd thought and felt the same things; however, as we talked, we returned to what our hearts knew to be true. This was Bodhi's plan for the growth of his soul, as well as ours, his siblings' and others', though to what extent we may never know until we too leave this life.

Just as my clients and I explore the purpose and lessons of events in past lives, we do so for our current lives as well. We return to the painful events that the soul and subconscious has held onto, gaining the needed clarity and insight. Then we do for the inner child (or past parts of self) what is most needed physically or through words, and we do the same forgiveness of others and of self. As we go to the in-between times we can be surrounded by pure love and understanding; we find "the why."

The exercises, coping skills, and dynamic practices I learned and used during my grief journey may seem like a lot. However, as I've seen with clients and myself, this is actually very important. At times some practices will work; other times, something else is needed. Sometimes it'll be necessary to use multiple tools in a day. Most important is developing the practices that allow a greater feeling of peace, sacredness, and well-being overall. Then, when the difficult parts of life hit, I can be okay when things aren't.

Something that I hadn't considered prior to Bodhi's death was using plant medicine, specifically mushrooms, for healing. I am very connected to Mother Earth, nature, and the elements, and I believe they provide us with everything we need to heal. In fact, I had already started looking at the research around psychedelics and their benefit in trauma treatment. Of course, I'd also heard the stories about people using them to get high, but they are so much more valuable than that, and, as I looked at what I needed to process the trauma of Bodhi's death, all options were on the table.

The mushrooms can be used in microdosing, or, in higher doses, for journeying. With this avenue, they are used with sacredness and intention. A friend provided the shamanic and ancestral connection and music, and with my background I was able to integrate all that I learned and experienced. It allowed me the space to feel safe, to let go of control, and to trust my soul to take me where I needed to go, to gain a greater connection to my Spirit Team, and to access the ancient and collective wisdom available to all of us. I, along with my shamanic friend, have since helped others integrate their own plant medicine journeys. No tool is a quick fix, so I encourage you to open your mind to the opportunities and possibilities available for alchemizing grief, transmuting trauma, and healing hurts. The work of Paul Stamets, as well as the documentaries *Fantastic Fungi* and *How to Change Your Mind* by Michael Pollen, are good resources about psychedelics. I would also suggest checking out Dr. Andrew Huberman's podcast, *Huberman Lab*, as he summarizes the research on psilocybin, MDMA, ketamine, and more.

I'm not sure I can fully put into words what I experienced on the journey or in the microdosing, but I believe the way to describe it is that it allowed me to be expansive. I have dived deeper into exploring past lives, as well as other areas that seemed farfetched before, such as parallel lives, galactic lives, and interdimensional lives.

I also became more open to connecting with my ancestors and the possibility of contact with ascended masters such as Jesus, Mother Mary, Mary Magdalene, Kuan Yin, Buddha, Sekhmet, Neith, Boudica, Princess Diana, and others. This has expanded my work as well. In my client sessions I incorporate scientific research and best practices with the spiritual, the mystical, and even the unknown or not fully understood. In addition, I have launched a podcast. I've written this book. I've created a lot of content since Bodhi's death and I allowed myself to become more vulnerable in what I shared.

I have always been aware of nature and the beauty surrounding me, but now I am able to slow down, let go of the need to rush, let go of the need to be busy and to produce every minute of every day. I let go of the worries and fear of judgment and share from my heart and from my life experiences.

My positive experience, along with the current research and the long history of the benefits of psychedelics, has also led me to return to working as a Licensed Clinical Social Worker. My hope is to one day get involved in that research and, ultimately, open a clinic of my own.

The journey has manifested in the physical with astounding signs, symbols, and synchronicities. As an example, after a session where I connected with my ancestors, I received the message to slow down and be more present. I have carried a lot of ancestral guilt because their lives were so difficult while I, though I've certainly had struggles, have never gone hungry or experienced poverty as they did. This holds me back from fully feeling my feelings or acknowledging the struggles. As I folded up my chair, there was a snail under it! It was a physical reminder from my ancestors that I can stay present, slow down, and acknowledge my own struggles while offering gratitude for all my blessings.

I also let go of the lingering doubts I had around the signs and symbols I had been receiving most of my life – from seeing my deceased aunt and sister as a child to seeing signs from my college boyfriend Mike in the aftermath of his death and everything we have experienced since Bodhi's death. One of the most amazing signs came in an online grief group Matt and I attended. In the beginning of the session, we were asked to write a letter to our baby, which we would then read to the group. It was very emotional for both of us, sharing and listening to each other's pain. Then the leader had us do a lighter exercise: a dessert word scramble. As we looked down the list, my heart stopped. Spelled out in one of the scrambles was Bryce – the name of my brother who had passed. My mind began to spin into all the things that had to happen for Bryce's name to appear at this moment, in this scramble, in this group, just when I most needed a reminder that our loved ones never truly leave us. Earlier that day I had taken the dogs to the veterinarian. As I sat waiting, I looked up and saw a picture of a dragonfly, at that exact moment a dog named Bodie was being checked in for his appointment. I will take all the signs and synchronicities my loved ones want to send!

I have accepted that I am enough just as I am and am now living my life from that place, instead of always feeling that I am failing and falling short.

I am trusting the path and trusting the journey more and more every day.

I have always known, but am even more certain, of the interconnectedness of us all. I am a connector and love to share the amazing people I know with the world. I started my podcast to share conversations with these incredible people, and if I can't help you then I'm sure I'll be able to send you to someone who can.

I began to explore astrology more deeply and study Human Design and the gene keys. Human Design has helped me understand myself and my place in the world so much that I have taken the courses to offer these readings to others. I know that it is all written in the stars and in our charts. Our plan is in place before we even get here so it makes sense to use the tools that help us access that information.

Merriam-Webster defines astrology as "the divination of the supposed influences of the stars and planets on human affairs and terrestrial events by their positions and aspects." Human Design is a sort of "user's manual";[5] it maps out your unique genetic design, including conscious and unconscious aspects, and provides simple tools to discover your truth. It can help you to improve the quality of your life,

---

[5] https://www.jovianarchive.com/Human_Design/Why

make decisions to improve your relationships and work life, and to meet challenges without getting overwhelmed.

According to Richard Rudd, author of *Gene Keys: Embracing Your Higher Purpose*, "Gene Keys weaves together a kaleidoscope of insights from fields as diverse as biology, theosophy, anthropology, mythology and indigenous wisdom."[6] Beyond all this, *Gene Keys* is a book designed to bring about personal transformation by actually influencing your DNA. In the tradition of many mystical texts, it has an uncanny habit of coming alive as you contemplate and probe its interwoven insights. Around the same time *Gene Keys* was being written, a whole new current of breakthroughs also took place in the sciences. The "new biology" was born by molecular biologists such as Bruce Lipton, who showed that our DNA is not pre-programmed as we used to believe but is a highly sensitive, open system that responds to both emotion and thought. Experiments have shown that the phosphates deep within our cells expand and contract according to the electromagnetic impulses of our environment. And the environment that has the greatest impact on us is the subtle quantum biofield generated by our unconscious attitude toward life. In other words, our consciousness creates our biological reality.

I have deepened my sessions to explore the in-between times when we are with Source and make our soul contracts. We look for our purpose and the lessons we are here to learn this time – usually very simple yet complicated things, like loving more, practicing self-love, forgiveness, and family.

I have received guidance from mediums and coaches. I joined a mastermind group hosted by Sunny Dawn Johnston and met some amazing ladies there. I had a Human Design session with a woman named Allison Cullen, through whom I met Alexandra Wyman, now a dear

---

[6] Rudd, Richard. (2013). *Gene Keys: Embracing Your Higher Purpose*. Watkins Publishing.

friend. We have been on each other's podcasts, presented at the International Association for Suicide Prevention in Piran, Slovenia, and I know we will continue to work together to help others heal mind, body, heart, and soul.

I highly recommend exploring your own gene keys and Human Design chart. As I learn more and more about our charts and the tools available, seismic shifts have occurred in how I view my life path. According to Rudd's book, my life's work is within the thirty-first gene key. The following excerpt illustrates how my life path has unfolded.

> *The Shadow is Arrogance, the Gift is Leadership and the Siddhi is Humility.*
>
> *The 31ˢᵗ gift of Leadership sits like the fulcrum of a seesaw between Humility the Siddhi and Arrogance the Shadow Language is the ultimate programming tool and shadow words can have a far deeper effect than presence since words endure forever.*
>
> *The real arrogance comes from being cut off from the divine source. Words that are not rooted in a profound sense of wonder are always, at some level, arrogant.*
>
> *You can only ever be free when you have escaped language. When the heart finally begins to speak, it organizes the words without you having to think about their meaning. The high frequency of the heart is what conveys true meaning. Arrogance then is an addiction to the words and language rather than the frequency of the intention that hides between and behind the words. All words, opinions and thoughts with which you identify are agents of the great illusion of your separate existence. There are two forms of arrogance. The repressive form manifests as false humility, and those are people who defer their power to others. False humility hides nothing more than fear. The reactive side to arrogance is based on anger. And emerges as a kind of haughty scorn.*

The gift of leadership is really a gift of influence. The gift is no longer caught up in the fear of what others think.

They want to help others break out of the very same matrix in which you yourself were once caught. To move beyond the intellect and into the heart your natural urge is to help others escape that suffering in some way.

True humility can only occur at the Siddhi frequency because it requires complete obliteration of individuality.

Because the 31st Siddhi is truly humble, it has no agenda. It is not necessarily interested in freeing people from their illusions, even though it may unwittingly do so. Such a being realizes that it is not possible to influence anyone in this world. It doesn't matter what such a person does in life. They are content to leave the world exactly as it is. Nonetheless, such a person still carries the same genetic coding that requires them to speak from the cutting edge of consciousness. The gift level self identifies with evolution. The siddhi says whatever it must say, knowing that the words come from the collective and go back to the collective.[7]

My greatest passion is to help people. It always has been, but now I have a greater awareness around assisting only if their answer is a yes. If not, I have to detach from it. I'm not the savior. I am the journey guide. It might be a short stop or a long one. You may know it's what you need, but not yet ready. There may be naysayers that may creep in and pull you away. You may not be interested in doing things differently or healing past hurts. It may hurt too much to look inward.

Yet, even when this is the case, I see people transform as the scales fall from their eyes. Their hearts heal and they can see themselves as they are meant to; they love, accept and forgive themselves. They move into

---

[7] Rudd, Richard. (2013). *Gene Keys: Embracing Your Higher Purpose.* Watkins Publishing.

a state of being. No more doing unnecessarily, but doing things only in alignment and if it is from their heart. Seeing the joy in the simple and seeing the beauty in all, even what would be dark and nasty to others. With me observing and speaking from the heart, they offer themselves the perspective shifts of what has happened to them in the past and how they had seen themselves. What they had known to be true is now different. I hold the space; I give the permission and, most importantly, I detach from "truth," because what is true today for me may change tomorrow, just as it might for the people sitting in front of me.

My wish is that you find what you most need on your healing journey so you can be even happier, more relaxed, more at peace, laughing more and having more fun. **The gift of death has allowed me to embrace this even more deeply. It's not a perfect journey, but it is worth it.**

Whether you take the journey with me or someone else, or on your own, look to the stars, look to nature, and, most importantly, look within your heart to find what speaks to you most.

CHAPTER 3

PRACTICES FROM BODHI

P lease read with an open mind to discern what exercises may benefit you. Mine have shifted and changed through each trial, so it's very beneficial to hear about many modalities.

We are constantly working to choose to laugh more and enjoy life more in honor of Bodhi. To love each other harder and honor the loss, but allow it to catapult us into living our best lives. My recent mantra has been, "Help me to be blessed, to see my blessings, and to bless others." We deserve to welcome the good stuff into our lives; I always want to be grateful for our beautiful life and I want to help others as I can. That can be a smile or a quick chat, as well as in the sessions that I offer for heart healing.

Throughout Bodhi's story, you've heard things I used for heart healing; now, I will share in depth the ways that helped me most when our son decided not to come to Earth. The two main ones are storytelling and a meditation to meet a loved one in Spirit.

There are many other ways we have chosen to honor Bodhi and the others that have transitioned to Spirit. One of those has been memorial tattoos, layered with meaning for me and my nearest and dearest who have died. You can find what means the most to you.

As we were nearing Bodhi's first birthday it felt like a struggle to know what to do. We have three other children and I didn't want to make it dark or heavy for them. We can allow the darkness, the heaviness, and the questioning at times, but that's not the place I want to live in. One morning I woke up with the idea of doing a birthday cake battle with a rainbow theme. This was in honor of the favorite poem we used on his memorial cards, "Look for Me in the Rainbows." Eric, a gifted photographer and my friend, was on board. We dressed in white, got rainbow confetti cannons, and made birthday cakes – each one a different color of the rainbow. The kids chose their colors and Bodhi got orange.

We brought his urn with his ashes and his picture.

We blew out his candle for him, we got competitive as we smashed cake on each other, laughing our way through it, those good belly laughs. We really leaned into feeling that we were using his short life for a greater purpose, to harness even more love for each other, more laughter, more fun and more joy.

Bodhi's first birthday celebration.

Now I ask you, where can you do the same?

Where can you harness more joy?

More laughter?

More fun?

I encourage you to do that in honor of those you have loved and lost, because they aren't really lost. They are here with us and we can develop a new relationship with them.

Honor them in the way that works for you. I will offer you many exercises throughout this book, but you will need to find your path. I often help clients process their grief and that looks different for everyone. When we set the intention of processing it in the way they most need to honor their loved ones, it's so powerful and transformative. The possibilities stretch out before them in beautiful and perfect ways they might not have thought or felt was possible prior to their session.

It might hurt to sit down and get quiet enough to actually feel and acknowledge your feelings, but I promise you it is worth it and it is possible. It is also what your loved ones most want for you.

One of the greatest gifts I was given as I've navigated grief was a guided meditation. And within that meditation I was able to connect with our son, Bodhi Grant. He showed me that I can weep over his grave and go down that dark tunnel, or I can turn around and see the beauty in all things.

We have all lost people we love. To help you connect with them, I offer this meditation with beautiful music from the memorial chimes from my Pappy's funeral by Chris and Nicole Kupchella (celebrateeverystep.com/bbd-bonus-meditation). Sit back or lie back and allow your mind, body, heart and soul to open to experience connection with them. It can be done for anyone of any religion or belief system to honor this special connection.

The Tool of Storytelling

Storytelling is very powerful. It has carried cultures from one generation to the next. However, storytelling can have a dark side. It can keep us stuck in old patterns and beliefs; it can even prolong pain and suffering. As mentioned earlier, grief stories tend to go one of two ways – either people "one up," saying their grief is worse than that of others, or they downplay everything. I would say things like, "Our baby died, but he was never born so your situation is worse because he was three months." Or, "Our baby died, but lots of people donated money and we were taken care of at the hospital." I can now hear the insanity in those words, but I had to catch myself and still do at times, especially, when I'm trying to make someone else more comfortable after mentioning Bodhi's death.

I have seen the power of storytelling without filters. Letting go of all the "yeah, buts," the "shoulds" and "coulds," or anything else that explains things away.

This is the exercise I am encouraging here. I want you to write your story without filters.

Place your feet on the ground and begin to notice your breathing getting a little slower, a little deeper, a little more even. Feel your belly soften as thoughts begin to slow. You can do this as you are reading the instructions and the questions. Begin to let go of expectations. Let go of analyzing the information that comes to you. Inviting in the white light of the Divine or other spiritual accompaniment. Feeling your heart opening and expanding.

Now, begin to allow your story to flow to you. And make note below. You may cry, scream, stomp, run or more – allow it, and then keep writing. If you have a therapist or trusted friend you may want them on standby. If you need support, schedule a session with me and we can work together to write and move the emotions up and through the body so it's no longer holding you back in any way.

As your story flows, allow the love and loss to flow too.

Say all the things you most need to say to your people who have crossed into Spirit.

They may even want to talk back to you; allow that now.

Get out the who, what, where, when, why and engage all your senses as you recall your life story.

If any of this feels like a struggle you may want to come back to this section after you have done the exercises in the rest of the book.

> Who am I?
>
> What's important to me?
>
> What were some of the happiest moments of my life?
>
> What were some of the saddest?
>
> How do I spend my time?
>
> What am I most proud of?
>
> What losses and grief do I feel (i.e., actual deaths, death of self, expectations)?
>
> What are the lessons I've learned along the way?
>
> What are the blessings that have come about?
>
> Do I allow myself to feel my feelings?
>
> How do I best allow emotion to move through me?
>
> Am I numbing or distracting?
>
> Has my body experienced any tightness, pain, or conditions in the aftermath of death or loss?
>
> What can still make me smile or feel happiness?
>
> Allow it all to come up and flow through you onto the paper and allow it to be transmuted into a healing practice for you.

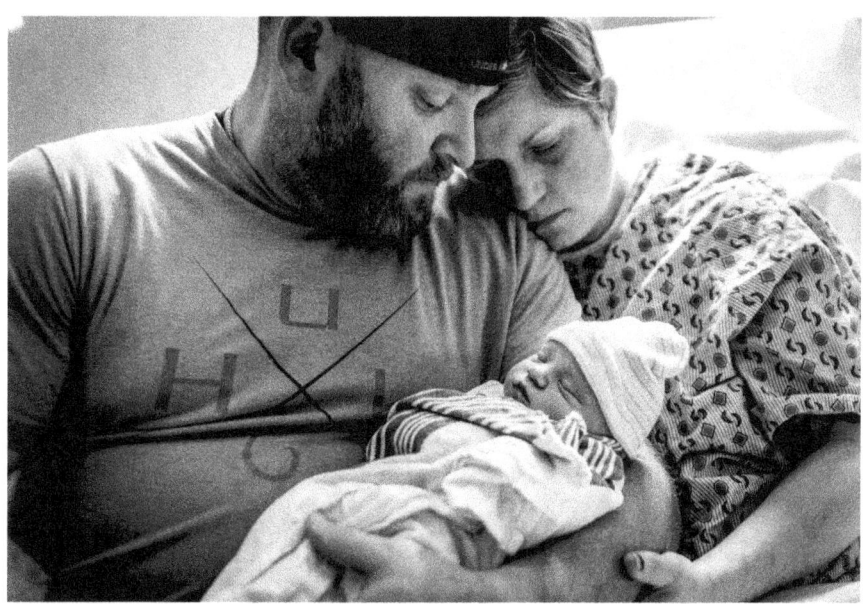

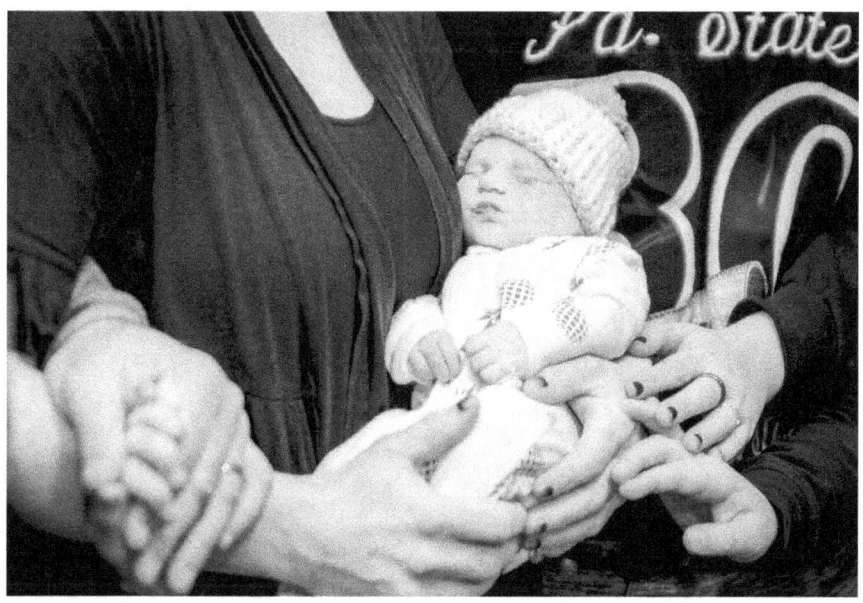

Bodhi and the hands of me, Matt, Issadoa, Jacob and Ian

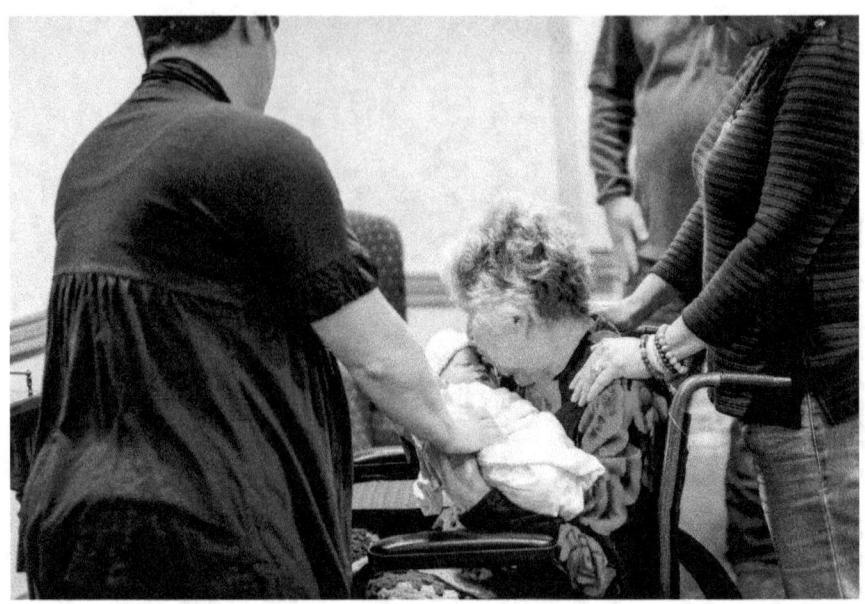

Matt's grandma, Bodhi's great grandma holding him

PART III

My Life Journey
Through Death

CHAPTER 4

MY SISTER CLAIRE

In 1985, my mom told me and my brother that she'd be having another baby. I can remember standing at the kitchen island back in the olden days when there was only one phone in the house and it was attached to a base, sometimes on the wall. She and my dad had my younger brother, and I called all our aunts, uncles, and grandparents to tell them the news. I was just three years old and yet I remember this so clearly. At that age I didn't really notice much about pregnancy, though we did talk about it. I had a little brother and lots of cousins, so I was familiar with babies and what that meant.

That fall, we celebrated my Great-grandma Shuagis's hundredth birthday. There was a big party and family and friends came in from all over the country. My oldest uncle, Uncle Marty, rented a video camera and went around interviewing everybody. His main objective was to interview my great-grandma, which was full of amazing details of traveling across the ocean and settling into a new country. I recently had it all digitized so I could watch the interviews. There is a segment where I and one of my cousins are up in my aunt and uncle's treehouse, looking out over the ledge. Uncle Marty asks us our names and how old we are, then he asks me what we should name the baby. My response was Theresa.

As I watched that, I had a big aha. I was four and my Aunt Theresa had died in 1968. But at four do you really even understand life and death and birth? I did, and it was a part of me that I had not fully consciously brought back into my awareness. But, watching that clip, I recalled being in certain places and noticing my Aunt Theresa, kind of on the edges. I called her my imaginary friend. At eight months old Theresa contracted pneumonia with a high fever that resulted in encephalopathy and severe mental retardation. They tried to care for her at home, but she became a danger to herself and others and was placed in a state hospital, where she was confined to a wheelchair, had her teeth pulled, and wore a football helmet. Her horrific life inspired several of her siblings, including my mom and Uncle Bobby, to go into special education teaching. Theresa serves as a reminder of the immense impact one person can have.

Grandma Szkeresh, Aunt Theresa and Grandpa Szekeresh

In October that same year, my mom and dad found out that the baby she was carrying had died. About eight months along in her pregnancy, she had to be induced and still go through the labor and delivery. They named her Claire. I remember my aunt coming to watch us while my mom was in the hospital. I can remember so vividly and clearly my idea to put up the Cabbage Patch birth certificates. (If you remember in the wayback machine, each Cabbage Patch Kid came with a birth certificate.) It boggles my mind that I understood at that age that when you have a baby you get a birth certificate. I always say kids are so perceptive!

If we slow down enough and watch the kids in our life, we can really marvel at their perceptiveness.

Amazingly, I can still remember the tiny casket, funeral home and cemetery. Years later, we'd see that casket again when my brother died. They exhumed Claire's vault and placed it on top of Bryce's in the same plot.

My mom had a box in her closet with a few pictures and a hospital bracelet. I would sneak and go look at it. I was so little and wasn't sure why that felt important and necessary; I just knew that it did.

Grandma Shuagis at her 100th birthday party. Standing behind her:
my mom (pregnant with Claire), Joshua, Dad, and me.

The Lessons and Blessings

After Claire died, I would see her and Theresa, especially at my grand-parents' house in the corner by the grandfather clock. I still called them my imaginary friends because I didn't understand who they were. Now I know they were showing up in spirit form. I can remember back then, feeling alone. I could be with people and still always felt alone and different from everyone else. Everything felt hard. As I think back to that struggle with my big emotions, not knowing what to do with them and the adults not knowing how to help me, I remember feeling so comforted that these "friends" were close by.

Now, in the work that I do, I connect people with their loved ones or pets that have crossed into Spirit. It can bring them a lot of comfort, just as it brought me comfort to know that those I loved were never far away.

In the second grade, I used to pray to die. It all felt like too much. When I transport myself back to that time, I remember getting ready for school every day in my blue plaid skirt and my white button-down shirt and my little penny loafers. I also remember feigning illness to the point that the teacher told me she had to see the throw up before I flushed it. I felt like I didn't fit in, I didn't feel liked. *In the second grade!* When I look at my own kids, it hits home even more that I was a baby, so young to be thinking and feeling like that.

I was always a very responsible kid. I don't know if it came from being the oldest or that was just my personality or part of my soul lessons – probably a combination of the three. I have always felt responsible for everyone else's well-being. Most, if not all, of the time, this was to my own detriment. I am finally at a place in my life where I do put myself first. I no longer see that as selfish, but actually necessary. I turned so hard away from being selfish that I went in the opposite direction. When you see people who think the world revolves around them, or that they're the center of the Universe, and that somehow everybody should say and do and be exactly what they want them to say, do and be, it shifts your brain. It felt so yucky to me that I went to the other extreme, wanting everybody around me to be happy at all times. I now know that's completely impossible. Number one, I am not responsible for anyone but myself; and, number two, you can't make everybody happy all the time.

If you will, imagine yourself in second grade, or maybe you have a child or grandchild that's seven or eight and think about how little they are. Are there any hurts within you from that time that need healing?

And think about me at that age, taking on the weight of the world. It's no wonder that it all felt like too much and that I would cry and ask to die. My son is nine now, and the thought of him feeling responsible for the world makes my heart hurt—though I can't help but laugh at how over the top I was. Or, maybe that was the childlike perceptiveness spilling out.

Practices for Claire and the Clairs

The Clairs are your intuition and spiritual senses. As you read through them, pay attention to how each one resonates with you. Which sense is usually your strongest? This allows you to improve your intuition. In my journey and in client sessions we work on releasing what holds someone back from fully trusting and believing in their connection to the other side, and in signs, symbols, and synchronicities. It could be that in church you were told divination is evil or your aunt told you using tarot cards was talking to the devil. Or you've been taught to not trust yourself through gaslighting or internalizing mistakes you've made.

I rely on my gifts of empathy, clairsentience, and claircognizance to tune into my clients' energy, vibrations, and the messages they most need. These gifts also assist me in helping them strengthen or tune back into their own intuition.

The following practice will help you to release anything that holds you back from tapping into your intuition before finding your strongest intuitive sense.

First, place your feet on the ground and begin to notice your breathing getting a little slower, a little deeper and a little more even. Feeling your belly soften and thoughts begin to slow. You can do this as you are reading the instructions and the questions. Beginning to let go of expectations. Letting go of analyzing the information that comes to you.

Now, begin to notice any fears or worries that hold you back from trusting your intuition. Write down your first answer and anything that flows to you.

Now that you've noticed them, it's time to let them go. As you breathe, give your mind, body, heart, and soul permission to release these old beliefs. You may release to earth, air, fire, water or Spirit in whatever way works for you.

Once you have tapped into and released, read through the Clair definitions and notice which resonate(s) most.

There are many online resources that provide the Clair definitions. These have been gathered from www.oprah.com/spirit/developing-your-5-clair-senses-rebecca-rosen/all.

Clairsentience means clear feeling.

This is the ability to perceive emotional or psychic energy that is imperceptible to the five standard senses. This entails feeling a person's or spirit's emotions or feeling another's physical pain. Many of us are clairsentient without consciously being aware of it. When we get a strong "gut" feeling, positive or negative, about someone we just met or when we get the "chills" for no apparent reason, we may be tuning into the emotional energy of a person or a spirit around us. Being highly sensitive and in tune, not only with our own feelings but the feelings of others, makes us natural healers and caregivers. We often feel inspired to pursue careers as doctors, therapists, counselors, nannies and teachers. If this is you, clairsentience is at the top of your senses list.

Claircognizance means clear knowing.

This is when we have knowledge of people or events that we "shouldn't" have knowledge about. Spirit impresses us with truths that simply pop into our minds seemingly out of nowhere. An example of this would be a premonition: a forewarning of something that will happen in the future. Claircognizance requires tremendous faith because there's often no practical explanation for why we suddenly "know" something. Many philosophers, professors, doctors, scientists, religious and spiritual leaders and powerful sales and business leaders tend to be highly intuitive and seem to just know the facts with a sense of certainty.

Clairaudience means clear hearing.

This is when we hear words, sounds, or music in our own mind's voice that are said to exist beyond the reach of ordinary experience or capacity, such as the voices of the dead.

On rare occasions, Spirit may be able to create audible (external to you) sound, though this takes a tremendous amount of focused energy. Some of us best retain and comprehend information when we hear it spoken aloud. Our natural talents tend to lie in our auditory faculties, often making us gifted musicians, singers, writers, and public speakers. If this feels right to you, clairaudience may be a leading sense for you.

Clairgustance means clear tasting.

This is the ability to taste something that isn't actually there – usually out of the blue. Oftentimes, a deceased loved one is attempting to communicate a memory or association we have with a particular food or beverage that reminds us of them. If we have a heightened sense of taste, this would make us natural chefs, bakers, or food critics.

Clairalience means clear smelling.

This is being able to smell odors that don't have any kind of physical source. Instances of this could include smelling the perfume or the cigarette smoke of a deceased relative, indicating that they are around us. When our sense of smell is strong and distinct, we may find that certain smells connect us to past memories, or we may be drawn to working as a florist, a wine taster, or a perfume fragrance creator.

Clairvoyance means clear seeing.

This is when visions of the past, present, and future flash through our mind's eye, or third eye, much like a daydream. It's the supernatural power of seeing objects or actions removed in space or time from natural viewing. Many of us are highly visual and able to understand an idea best when we see it written or sketched out as an image on a computer screen or canvas. Visual people often choose to be artists, builders, photographers, decorators, designers, and so forth. If this sounds familiar, your clairvoyance is most likely a dominant sense.

Make note of your strongest sense and begin to practice and play with that sense. Make a consistent practice of recognizing and acknowledging that strongest sense and strengthening the others.

CHAPTER 5

MY GRANDMA KUPCHELLA

M y grandma died when I was in ninth grade. I got called to the office and was told only that my aunt was picking me up. I sat on the steps, waiting and knowing something had happened. When she arrived, she told me that Grandpa Kupchella had found my grandmother that morning – she had passed in her sleep. The family was shocked, for she'd had lots of health issues and many surgeries over many, many years, she wasn't sick at the time; plus, she was only sixty-seven. I recall how old this seemed to my fourteen-year-old self, and of course, I have a different perspective now that I am forty-three. I also vividly remember leaving the viewing to go out to the car and sleep. This was the first time I used sleep as a healing tool, but would come to use it many more times as difficult things transpired. There were so many things about our relationship that were special, and so many ways in which she influenced my life.

Dora Kupchella looked like the stereotypical Eastern European immigrant depicted in the 1980s, with short, permed hair that was always done perfectly and covered with a nice cloth babushka when she went out (a plastic one when it rained). For me, she was just Grandma Kupchella, a soft place to land, a source of comfort. She was also the one who let me dye my hair red and bought me a black bra. Recently, I was blessed with the opportunity to reminisce about her with her sister, who was nearing her ninety-fifth birthday. I'm so thankful I talked with my great-aunt, because she died shortly after our meeting.

My grandmother didn't talk a lot about her younger years, but I knew there must have been something to the story because her mom lived longer than she did and I never met her. Apparently, there had been a falling-out long before my time. I've since come to learn that my great-grandma was a pretty mean person, that she may have even tried to push my grandma down the stairs when she was really young. From the stories, it seems likely that she had some mental illness or other issues, but that was before treatment with medications or therapy. Such things were kept secret and pushed down into the deepest, darkest recesses of our minds and souls.

A far happier story, and a favorite of mine, was how my grandparents met. Like so many other young men of his generation, my Grandpa Kupchella enlisted at age eighteen and was sent to Europe to serve in World War II. As soldiers did not have a lot of opportunity to communicate with their loved ones, they would film reels that were later shown in local movie theaters back in the States.

One evening, his mother went to the movies, and after it was over, they showed one of those reels highlighting some of the soldiers and what was happening. Suddenly, there on the screen, she saw her son, John Kupchella, coming out of a church.

"My son, my son!" she cried out, "That's my son!"

Actually, she had four sons in the War and until that moment she hadn't known if they were alive or dead. It's unimaginable in today's world, but back then it was the norm.

In another part of the theater, Dora, who was sitting with her sister, also had a reaction when saw John Kupchella on the screen.

"I'm gonna marry that man," she said.

Now, in those days people tended to stay close to home and marry someone from their own town. Dora and John lived in different areas, but "coincidentally," when he returned from the war he and his best friend went to a dance in her town. Dora and her sister were there too, and you can guess what happened – or at least part of it. John and his friend married those sisters and built lives with them. On a soul level John and Dora knew they would come together; that's why she looked at that screen and saw a future husband and why he felt the tug to go to a dance several towns away.

From early childhood I spent a lot of time with my grandma. Each morning before kindergarten I would go to their house, which was right down the street, then return after the school day for lunch and to watch *The Price is Right*. She'd sit in her recliner, her latest romance novel sitting on the glass lamp table, painting her nails with Sally Hansen's Hard As Nails strengthening formula. I can still smell that smell! My grandpa would come and go; he was always an active and busy guy.

I went to that school all the way up to eighth grade, and my grandparents' home remained my go-to anytime I wasn't feeling well. In second grade, when I was really struggling with my emotions and often crying and claiming I was sick, I would get to go to their house, drink some ginger ale, eat some saltines, watch Bob Barker on the tube and just be surrounded by her love, care, and attention.

Great Uncle Mike and Great Aunt Dottie, my grandma's sister.
Dora and John Kupchella, my grandma and grandpa.

Me, Grandpa Kupchella and Grandma Kupchella in fancy hats.

The Lessons and Blessings

Hearing old stories about my grandma made me realize where my feistiness comes from. She did not put up with any crap! My great-aunt shared a story of them walking home one evening. A man was following them and bothering them and even spit in their direction. And Grandma let him have it! This was in the 1940s, when women didn't speak up and were still considered property. But she saw women's value differently and paved the way for others to see the world differently as well.

While my grandpa was at war he prayed and promised that if he made it home alive, he would go to church every Sunday. He had many harrowing incidents – he even got shot in the chest and his Bible stopped the bullet! After making it home safely, he kept his promise, attending every Sunday Mass and every holy day. My grandma went with him unless she was sick or recovering from surgery, and she always prayed the novenas. Grandpa lived to ninety-six and continued going to church. Catholic practices were a big part of my grandparents' daily lives, and they were also a significant part of my upbringing.

Grandpa would poke me in the back anytime I was hunched over and say, "Sit up straight, stand up straight." To this day, whenever I spend too long hunched over the computer or my phone, I can still feel that finger in my back and hear his voice in my head. He probably said this because Grandma had a hunched back and he wanted me to avoid that.

She had started having neck and back surgeries when my dad and his siblings were still at home. She'd also had two near-death experiences – one where she crossed over to the other side and one where she saw that white light. One of those times she saw her dad across a field and started making her way to him, but he stopped her and let her know that she had a choice. She could go with him or she could come back, and in that moment she chose to come back.

I heard about those experiences when I was little, but I didn't realize what exactly they meant. They just seemed like cool stories and felt very true to my soul. My grandma would visit mediums, tea leaf readers, and other seers. I think that came from understanding that there was more than what we could see with our eyes. She found comfort in her Catholic faith, but she also found comfort in having heart-to-heart conversations with others who were more in tune with the Spirit world. After hearing many stories from her sister and from my aunts, I now believe that she too had the "second sight," which was how intuition was referred to back then.

I get asked all the time about how and why I became interested in past life regressions, and I tell them it was because of my grandma. Another story she shared was when she and my grandpa went to San Francisco – the first time for both of them. But somehow, Grandma knew how to get around. She knew exactly where she was and where to turn to get to where they needed to go.

What's the explanation for that?

How would she know how to navigate a city she had never been to? She attributed it to having been to or living there in a past life.

Of course, when I was younger, I didn't really know what that meant. Again, it was just something that felt possible; her story had expanded my awareness and my view of the world without me even knowing it at the time.

Practices from Grandma Kupchella

Exercise #1 Letting Go of Definites

As I reflect on the many blessings and lessons my grandma offered me, one remains at the forefront: she was a refuge when my emotions and being in the world felt like too much.

The death of self she provided was a death of black-and-white think-ing, of definites and certainties. This enabled me to open to the possi-bilities of the Spirit world and our innate ability to regain and maintain a connection with it.

When you have a near-death experience, you recognize that things may not be what they always seem on the surface. When you are in a place you've never been before, yet you know all the streets, it makes you question what you believe to be true. And that's actually a good thing.

The world is a different place because of people like Grandma Kup-chella. That's the type of person I want to be. I want to be a person who questions, a person who looks inward for how to live and interact with others. This quest for constant growth and evolution has helped me build a career as a past life regressionist and hypnotherapist, even though I live in a place where such practices are not the norm—and, in fact, are sometimes seen as evil or the devil's work by some.

The really beautiful part of my willingness to buck the norm is that I have witnessed transformation in others. This transformation occurred because they saw what was true within themselves reflected in their experiences in current life hypnosis, past life regression, or galactic or interdimensional life explorations. They feel seen and understood, maybe for the first time in their lives. They acknowledge that there is more than just what we can see with our physical eyes and that brings them a deep peace.

That said, I do have a tendency toward black-and-white thinking – a shadow side for me because so much of life falls in the gray. The gray is where the magic lives, where things don't have to be certain and defi-nite, where possibilities are endless, and where life is limitless. The gray is where I can trust that my Spirit Team, my loved ones, my Ancestors, my Guides, my Angels, and my animal friends are there for me. Where

I can understand that we are energy first and foremost, and that we will return to energy from our human forms. That we can communicate with the other side while we are here. And, most of all, we can live from a place of love.

Coming from that place makes it easier to do things differently from the way they've always been done. For example, you can express a difference of opinion with someone without anger. We can disagree, we can think differently, we may even choose to live our lives differently, and we can love each other through that process. There must be mutual respect and kindness, and if there isn't then it's okay to speak up. It's necessary to stand in your strength and in your power.

Compassion and empathy are vital for our soul's growth and expansion. We've all had lifetimes where we've been the "bad person," and there is a lesson and a purpose in that.

This is where we might learn compassion and empathy. Berkley uses the term "empathy" to describe a wide range of experiences. Emotion researchers generally define empathy as the ability to sense other people's emotions, coupled with the ability to imagine what someone else might be thinking or feeling.

Brené Brown outlines four steps: perspective taking (putting yourself in someone else's shoes); staying out of judgment and listening; recognizing emotion in another person that you have may have felt before; and communicating that you can recognize that emotion. Empathy allows us to acknowledge that, given the same circumstances someone else is in, we could have done the same thing.

> **"Peace is a daily, a weekly, a monthly process, gradually changing opinions, slowly eroding old barriers, quietly building new structures."**
>
> **~ John F. Kennedy**

Take a few moments to look at that for yourself. Place your feet on the ground and begin to notice your breathing getting a little slower, a little deeper, a little more even. Feel your belly soften and thoughts begin to slow. You can do this as you are reading the instructions and the questions. Begin letting go of expectations, letting go of analyzing the information that comes to you, and inviting in the white light of the Divine or other spiritual accompaniment.

And now, begin to ask yourself these questions and allow the answers to flow to you, writing your first answer.

> Where can I let go of societal norms and find what's true for me?
>
> What box have I put myself in or labels have I put on me?
>
> What box or labels have those around me put me in or put on me?
>
> Where can I expand my view of others or the world?
>
> Where can I grow in compassion and empathy?
>
> As I feel into my heart and soul, how do I want to be living my life?

I'm forever grateful that my grandma was a safe place to land and loved me for who I was, just as I was. I thank her for helping me expand my understanding that there's more to this world than what we can see with our physical eyes. This all came about because she experienced that and made the impossible real for me. Let's open you to more possibilities in your connection too.

When I was little, Grandma told everybody she quit smoking. But really, she would just go to the bathroom, open the window and turn on the fan, thinking none of us could smell those menthol cigarettes. Now, I am fond of that smell; in fact, it is one of my reminders that she is near.

Exercise #2 Using the Senses to Connect

Smells are especially powerful for me. For others there may be other senses that are stronger. Smells evoke memories. I see a lot of people for whom smells evoke a flashback of a traumatic event. I used so much witch hazel after Bodhi's death it still gives me a jolt of emotion when I get a whiff.

On the other hand, smells can also evoke good memories that make our souls sing and bring back the people and times we miss. Whenever I went toward my grandma's bedroom on the way to the bathroom, I would stop to look at her jewelry. (I still love a good shiny piece of jewelry or a gemstone.) I'd then head to look at all the little bottles she had on her counter – how I loved them! – along with her compacts, face creams and nail polishes and powders galore. She had one powder in a pretty compact, and I can still smell its scent mixed with that cigarette smoke; every now and then I'll get a whiff of it and know that she's around. The other thing I remember from being in her bedroom was the sound of mourning doves outside the window. Even now, when I hear the mourning doves that sit in a pair on the line above my yard, I think of her. Whether I'm going out to sit on my rock and meditate, or take out the dogs in the morning or my one cat that loves to go outside, the doves' *coo...coo* takes me right back to that safe, warm feeling I had whenever I was with my grandma.

Using the senses is an important way to look for and maintain that connection to our loved ones in Spirit. Of course, we still miss them when they cross over, but they do stay with us and make their presence known in so many different ways. The more present we are in the moment, the more we can see those signs and symbols and synchronicities all around us. So join me in getting present and deepening your connection.

Take some time in this moment to open up all of your senses and connect with your present environment. Noting what you are seeing, smelling, hearing, even tasting. What do you physically feel? What do you emotionally feel in this moment? Sometimes I'll even stomp my feet to get really present.

If it feels right, you may want to invite a loved one in Spirit to join you and notice all your senses in relation to them.

Place your feet on the ground and begin to notice your breathing getting a little slower, a little deeper, a little more even. Feel your belly soften and thoughts begin to slow. You can do this as you are reading the instructions and the questions. Begin letting go of expectations, letting go of analyzing the information that comes to you, and inviting in the white light of the Divine or other spiritual accompaniment.

Now, begin to ask yourself these questions and allow the answers to flow to you, writing your first answer.

> What sound do you hear as your loved one is near? This could be their actual voice, a message from them, a favorite song, or a sound like the doves that remind me of my grandma.
>
> What smell do you smell as your loved one is close? It could be the smell you associate with them or a symbolic smell such as roses for your Aunt Rose.
>
> What does it evoke in your mind? Is there anything that you are seeing in your mind's eye? It could be a color, their actual form or another sign or symbol for them.
>
> Are there any tastes you notice that remind you of your loved one? It could be a favorite meal or even something like the flavor of their cigarette or cigar.
>
> Is there anything you feel physically in your body when they are near? It could be a tingle, a pressure, even the feeling of a hug or hand on your face.

What emotions or feelings do you experience when you invite them close? It could be a wave of peace, love, or security.

If painful memories are attached, it's okay; there are ways to do healing around them. In my sessions we go back to the time these events occurred and gain clarity and insight, understand the purpose or lessons, offer forgiveness to others, and, most importantly, to ourselves. We offer comfort and soothing to our inner self in the way that we didn't receive when we needed it; we offer the messages that are soothing and healing to our soul. As we go to the in-between times we can be surrounded in pure love and understanding and find the why and purpose. It is truly powerful and so healing.

Is there anything they'd like to say to you?

Anything you'd like to say to them?

What message will you bring back with you?

Really breathe in that love and peace and understanding as you close out your session and gently open your eyes.

Exercise #3 Intergenerational Healing

Intergenerational patterns and traumas include the old stories and behaviors passed down to us. Some examples are: negative relationships, such as the strained bond with your mother that she had with hers; physical, mental, or sexual abuse; stories around money—or the lack thereof; repeating patterns in partner relationships; or even past-life traumas. It is possible to heal and let go of what no longer serves you in your current life. Sometimes, ancestral healing will be done between family members you never even knew. There are many possibilities to explore. Often overlooked are the *gifts* passed down through the generations, and we will explore this aspect as well in the exercise below.

Place your feet on the ground and begin to notice your breathing getting a little slower, a little deeper, a little more even. Feel your belly soften and thoughts begin to slow. You can do this as you are reading the instructions and the questions. Begin letting go of expectations. Letting go of analyzing the information that comes to you. Inviting in the white light of the Divine or other spiritual accompaniment.

And now, begin to ask yourself these questions and allow the answers to flow to you, writing your first answer.

> What are the old stories and patterns I'd like to release? What thoughts or beliefs have held me back?
>
> Who are the beings that will work with me on this particular healing work?
>
> What needs to be released from my body, mind, heart, and soul?
>
> Who do I need to forgive, including myself?
>
> What do I need to say to them or them to me?
>
> What tools or practices do I need to implement?
>
> What boundaries do I need to place for myself and my relationships to bring more healing and peace to my life?
>
> What ancestral gifts will I bring back to my current life?

Take a few moments to offer gratitude to your highest Self and your Ancestors for the guidance and experience today. You are now free to move forward, continuing to honor, love, and accept yourself to the highest possible degree every day.

CHAPTER 6

MY COLLEGE BOYFRIEND MIKE

I've quit a lot of things over the years because of unrealistic expectations, of not thinking I was worthy of the goodness in my life.

When I went to college I left behind my high school boyfriend, who was stable, safe, and solid, and started dating a wild guy who did things like snort pain pills and pierce his own nipples. And when that relationship ended, I turned all that hurt inward, criticizing myself. I felt like I didn't want to live anymore. I hadn't yet found the magic of playing rugby and the amazing ladies who would become my very best friends. It wasn't actual death I needed, it was a death of a narrow view of the world, a death of the narrow view of myself. When that happened, I was able to see possibility and opportunity. Everything was on the table and the world had opened up, which led to my connection with Mike and my adventure abroad.

In the summer between my junior and senior years I went to England with a friend. We stayed with her family in Birmingham and traveled to London and Amsterdam and other nearby places. It was great fun, but I needed money to finance our outings. After trying my hand at housekeeping at a hotel – a complete disaster – I fortunately found a job at a pub in the small town just outside the city.

The pub's manager was enthralled with Elvis and every karaoke night he would perform one of the King's songs. His rendition of "All Shook Up" still plays in my mind every now and then. There were several other bartenders, and they welcomed me with open arms, having a blast every night. The pub was filled with the local young people, bar regulars, and occasional travelers passing through town. They spoke English with accents so thick it was a couple of weeks before I understood an order for a pint of lager.

As my time there was winding down, I started planning a trip to Ireland and Scotland, but that would come to an abrupt end. One mid-August night, close to closing time, Graham yelled out, "The phone's for you." I assumed it was my friend calling to make plans for after work. Who else would even know how to call me here at the pub?

When I got to the phone, I could barely hear the voice on the other end. The later the night got, the noisier the bar became, with the jukebox going and people shouting to be heard over it. The clanging and clinking of glasses. That standard pub cacophony. With my finger in one ear, I moved around the corner, though there was only so far I could go because this phone was still on a cord attached to the wall. After a few minutes of alternately yelling and straining to listen, I realized it was my mom's voice on the other end. My heart sank then, because I knew something had happened. I could have never guessed what it was.

Mike, my on-again, off-again college boyfriend, had been in an accident. His friend was pronounced dead at the scene and Mike was put on life support, but my mom was telling me that the next day they were taking him off the ventilator...after they harvested his organs. I felt like the bottom dropped out of my world. That extreme noise I had been fighting against just minutes prior completely fell away and I felt like I was in a dark, silent tunnel of disbelief.

I hung up the phone, not knowing what I was going to do or what it even meant. We closed the bar, then, as we did every night, we sat down to drink and smoke cigarettes. I sat there and began to cry and tell my new friends what had happened. They knew I must have received bad news, but it was too loud to tell them until the pub cleared out.

I don't think I stopped crying for a minute, even as I swung into action. I booked a plane ticket back to the States. I quit the pub. I canceled the trip I was supposed to be going on to Ireland and Scotland. I threw all my stuff in a huge duffel bag and made my way to London, which was a good distance from Birmingham, to find the underground (subway) was closed. I seriously considered leaving my bag on the street because it was so heavy and I had been lugging it for so long. I was so physically, mentally, and emotionally drained. Somehow, I made it to the airport and onto the plane. As we soared high over the Atlantic, I cried and wrote a letter to Mike that I planned on placing in his coffin, as long as it was okay with his mom. It seemed the tears would never end.

I had flown into New York because it was the only flight that would get me back in time to the funeral. As we stood up to begin getting off the plane, a gentleman came up to me and said, "That boy that you're writing to, he loves you." Suddenly, I was back in that tunnel of silence. The noise of people collecting their belongings and talking with their travel companions about where they needed to go and what they needed to do completely fell away. And, in the moment, in that dark tunnel of silence, I was okay and everything was right with the world. A wave of peace and love washed over me, and even though I was still devastated I felt more able to handle the funeral and burial and aftermath. And I was so grateful for that first sign from Mike.

There were many assaults on my senses on that first leg of the journey. As we made our way to the baggage claim I couldn't see because I had been crying so hard. I managed to grab my duffle and stooped down, planning on retrieving my contact stuff, when I was quickly greeted by a security guard with an assault rifle. He told me I wasn't allowed to open my bag. This was in 2002, not long after the September 11th attacks. Somehow, I made it out of there, found my parents who had come to get me, and we began the six-hour drive to our town in Pennsylvania.

When I got to the funeral home for the viewing, I saw lots of people I knew from high school and from my college rugby team, but I could only focus on Mike's mom, dad, brothers, and him in the casket. As I made my way toward it, I found myself in that dark tunnel again; everything and everyone around me just dropped away and I could feel that deep peace. I placed that letter in the casket and talked to him within my mind and within my heart. But I had already said everything I needed to say. I don't remember speaking to anybody else.

A few months later, another mind-blowing sign happened. I was living at my parents' house until I headed back to school in a few weeks. I opened the cabinet and about fell over when I saw the bright blue bowls sitting there. "Mom," I asked, "where did these bowls come from?" I had given Mike the same bowls because he was eating out of Tupperware in his college apartment. Mom had no idea. We have a big family; people come in and out, bringing things and leaving others, but I knew without a doubt that these bowls, identical to the ones I'd bought in a different town, were a sign from him.

A few months later, while visiting home, I went to see Mike's spot in the mausoleum. As I drove away, my heart felt heavy; he should have been back in college and living his life, like I was. Suddenly, a song came on the radio that I had never heard prior and have never heard since. The artist was singing that heaven was all around us and, in all things, just the message I needed to hear. At the end of the song, there was a spoken line that didn't seem like it was part of the song so it really caught my attention: "I once knew a boy named Michael." Again, that tunnel descended and that whoosh of silence closed in. I've never been able to find that song again, but it allowed me to acknowledge what I knew to be true: our loved ones are just changing form, they do remain with us, they do see us, they do love us, and the possibility of connection remains.

The Lessons and Blessings

I was blessed by knowing Mike and his death taught me deeper life lessons.

Mike taught me to have and be more fun, to be more spontaneous and to be strong in who I am. This brought about a death of worrying about what others say or think of me.

Before I met Mike I was a major people-pleaser. I'd do things I knew weren't right or what I wanted to be doing because I wanted to be accepted and liked. Mike was the first person I felt accepted me, faults and all. I'm not proud to admit that I took advantage of that. I treated him poorly because I knew he wouldn't leave and it was my way of feeling powerful when I had so often felt disempowered and didn't like myself. Our adolescence and early twenties are times of self-discovery, but it can feel uncomfortable to go back and examine through the lens of our older, wiser selves. Doing that, however, is an important piece of growth and expansion, as is honoring the fact that I was truly doing my best, even if now it horrifies me. I realized I must give myself some grace and self-forgiveness, and offer gratitude for an experience that propelled me into being super strong in who I am and what I stand for. As a result, I no longer care, in a good way, what anyone thinks of me.

As we examine past relationships, we can get caught up in what could or would have been. But that doesn't allow us to be present in a current relationship – be it romantic, platonic, or professional or familial. It's that age-old adage of the grass being greener. I've seen this in client sessions: a false belief that someone else was "meant for them" and a sense of regret. Then, during a meditation, Mike came and said that if he had stayed alive it could have affected my current relationship. Wow, what a blow to think that I could have gone down a tumultuous path and ruined an amazing relationship. It snapped me into viewing things as they truly are, from a higher perspective. Divine wisdom can really give us a glimpse into these alternate realities and allow us to give thanks for what is, rather than longing for something different.

Practices from College Mike

Signs, symbols and synchronicities are the ways that our loved ones and Spirit Team let us know that we aren't alone, that we are loved and supported in all things. That we can ask them for intervention and help along the way, big and small. As you read above, I received many from Mike. There might even be past-life connections or synchronicities when you look back after death.

Years later, during a past life regression, I discovered an even deeper layer with Mike. In this meditation I had set the intention of exploring why I am obsessed with waterfalls. As I went back into the past life I saw myself as the youngest daughter, after a line of sons, of a Lord and Lady. Because of this they essentially locked me into my rooms for safety. I spent most of my time alone looking out my windows and over the fields of wildflowers and a little further off was a stream with a gurgling waterfall. I would spend hours watching water run over the rocks and the change in the seasons. Later on in that life I was married to a neighboring family's son in an attempt at bringing peace. However, that husband eventually had me beheaded. I know that sounds traumatic, but when viewing past lives we do feel the feelings and make note of what is important, but it is not harmful, it just gives insight and the opportunity for healing and expansion.

Another piece of that relationship was physical fitness. I met him through playing rugby, but as we talked, I realized that I had gone to aerobics classes with his mom for a couple of years. One time I was complaining about having gained weight; college food and beer will do that. He commented that if I just ran a little, I would easily lose the weight. I still laugh when I think of that comment, but at the time I was so mad because my weight and relationship to food had always been problematic, mostly with binging and obsessive thoughts around food. There are no coincidences and those that come into our life can highlight and help us heal old wounds, sometimes by saying things we don't want to hear, but need to hear.

On one date, Mike and I went to see the movie *John Q*. It's about a man who takes a hospital ER hostage after learning that insurance will not cover his son's heart transplant. It was a very intense film and sparked a conversation about organ donation on the way home. A very strange conversation for a twenty- and a twenty-one-year-old! Mike and I agreed that it was a no-brainer; in fact, we were both signed up to donate upon our deaths so someone else could live. Of course, we never thought something would actually happen, but upon Mike's death his parents did donate his organs. Because he was on life support, they were able to help and save so many lives.

Another special way our loved ones send signs is through dreams or visitations. There is a difference between a dream and a visit while in a dream state. You typically wake up from a visit remembering the interaction in detail, as opposed to a standard dream, where those details often slip away.

Twenty years later I still have a vivid memory and the feelings from Mike's visit. He walked into my basement apartment, hugged me, and said that he had been looking for me. He kissed my cheek and then it ended. But the deep feelings of peace and love and the sensation of his hug remain.

If your loved one comes to visit offer them some gratitude and remember that you can continue to tap into the physical and emotional feelings they impressed upon you and the messages you received.

In a similar vein are intuitive nudges to reach out to someone. I've had this happen many times since Mike's death, where someone pops into my mind that I haven't thought of in a while. When I reached out, they really needed that simple hello, thinking of you, message. It never hurts to act on it, even if someone thinks I'm weird, I'd rather let them know they are loved, valued and thought of than worry about that.

Mike was true to himself and all in, all the time. His death opened my heart and soul to noticing and acknowledging signs, symbols and synchronicities. Music has always been healing for me and him communicating his presence through a song strengthened that musical connection. Let's spend some time exploring that for you in a guided meditation and hypnosis practice I do often with people who come to alchemize their grief.

We all want to know that our loved ones haven't left us. We can see them in the signs, symbols and synchronicities, but it can feel hard to trust that.

I am a lover of music. And our loved ones or Spirit Team can communicate through music. I shared above how the song came on as I left Mike's grave that reminded me he was close.

Music has been extremely important to me when processing grief. I have a special playlist with one or more songs for each person I have lost, songs that remind me of them. When I'm running or when I'm driving, and in that more meditative flow state I listen to those songs. I call those people back in and close to my heart. I'll share some of those songs with you. Some of them may help you as well. Some have allowed me to get the anger out. Some allow me to get sadness out. Some just help me to feel really good. Others bring back those favorite memories. And singing or humming along soothes the vagus nerve, which soothes the nervous system.

I use music as a tool within our family too. My kids have wildly varied tastes and they get to choose songs on the way to school. We are learning to respect other's tastes even if they aren't our own. We also use it to reset energy after the inevitable frustrations and upsets of family life and getting out the door for school.

Other forms of sound can be healing and soothing to our nervous system and soul. Sound healing using crystal bowls or chimes, binaural beats, Solfeggio tones, and certain music have built in healing frequencies. I have used all of these and even delved into ecstatic dance to add to the Somatic release.

Oftentimes there are traumas surrounding a loved one's death, and that is all our brains can remember. I have witnessed and experienced the power of healing those traumas and shifting into the good memories – both happy and sad – that you shared together. This process brings them to the forefront so you can hold that vision of your loved one in the way that means the most to you.

Try this exercise on your own, or if you feel you need guidance you can contact me for a session.

Place your feet on the ground and begin to notice your breathing getting a little slower, a little deeper, a little more even. Feeling your belly soften and thoughts begin to slow. You can do this as you are reading the instructions and the questions. Beginning to let go of expectations. Letting go of analyzing the information that comes to you.

In your imagination, notice yourself on a path in a sacred, healing forest, or create your own scene. Feeling the warmth of the sun shining through the trees, seeing the shades of green in the leaves and moss and pines, smelling the deep earthy smell of the woods, brushing your hand along the rough bark.

As you make your way to a clearing in the trees, you feel the connection growing.

You can invite your loved one into this space with you. And now move through all of your senses. Notice how you see them; it could be a full form, or a shape or a color. How do you hear them? It could be their voice or another sound. How do you smell them? What tastes can remind you of them? A favorite meal? And how do you feel them? A physical sensation? A tingling, the pressure of a hug, or something else? And what emotions do you have when they are near?

Make note of what you experienced. There is no right or wrong way.

And now begin to ask yourself these questions and allow the answers to flow to you, writing your first answer.

> Where and how can I be more true to myself? What makes me happy in this moment?
>
> What would make me happy moving forward?
>
> What can I do in this moment that would allow a true smile to emerge?
>
> How can I love myself more?
>
> How can I be a better friend to others and to myself?

And now bring to mind your very favorite songs. These can be for you. And these can be in remembrance of those now in Spirit.

Make note of them.

> What memories or events do I need to release today?
>
> Where do I notice them in my mind, body, heart or soul?
>
> Breathing into that space and releasing to the sacred forest or Divine now.

Do I need to forgive anyone, including myself or does anyone need to forgive me?

What do I need to say to them or them to me?

And now allowing yourself to go to your very favorite memories with your loved one in spirit.

Make note below and allow that to be how you remember them moving forward.

Do this as many times as you wish.

You can access my *Blessed by Death* playlist using the link below, but I'll share with you here which songs I chose and why.

For Bryce, "Friends in Low Places" from our cousin's wedding karaoke, and "Spirit in the Sky" from *Remember the Titans*, his favorite movie (in fact, he borrowed a scene to use as his monologue when he auditioned for the school play, and we used it for his IUP funeral service).

For Bodhi, it's "Tears in Heaven"; "Heal Me"; and "The River," which I played during labor and after his death, reminding me to let things flow.

There is also "Never Break" to remind me that Matt and I can make it through anything. "Bigger than the Whole Sky" and "Snow on the Beach" were songs I used for release in the aftermath of his death, especially in Sedona.

For other family remembrances, and just to release emotion, I have "If You're Going Through Hell, Cry Your Heart Out"; "You're on Your Own, Kid"; "Save Me"; "Greenwine"; "Hurt"; and "When I look to the Sky." I have "Hallelujah" and "Amazing Grace" for Grandma Kupchella; "Send Me a Song" for Aunt Bernie; and For Aunt Rose, "The Dance."

For College Mike and our Indiana University of Pennsylvania (IUP) rugby team, "Boys on the Docks"; and for Uncle Bert, I have "I Run for Life."

Also included are some singalong songs to uplift my mood: "Little Talks," a favorite to sing with people doing different parts; "Beautiful Things"; "What's Up"; "The Long Run"; "My Joy is Heavy"; "Do the Dance"; "Beer Never Broke My Heart"; "Believer"; "Shine"; and "Sisyphus."

Some other meditation and heart-opening music is the Archangel Michael Protection, "Open Your Chakra"; "Heal Your Body"; and "Archangel Jophiel."

I hope you enjoy the songs as much as I do!

celebrateeverystep.com/bbd-bonus-spotify

CHAPTER 7

MY UNCLE BERT

In 2007 Matt and I were still living in Lexington, Kentucky after I finished my Masters in Social Work. For holidays and parties, we would head to the Cincinnati, Ohio area to visit my Uncle Bert, Aunt Colleen, and my cousins, as this was closer than driving to PA. Since my family is so large, certain relatives were more involved in my early years than others. My Uncle Bert was one of them. He and my aunt had three kids – their oldest and I were only a year apart; Bryce and their middle son were the same age, as were my younger sister and their youngest. We spent almost every Sunday together, plus time in between playing and eating meals.

Uncle Bert blessed me with the gift of running, the power of movement, and of learning about energy work, like reiki. He had that tough Hungarian exterior, but within him his big heart shone through. He was tough on us, but you knew that he loved you, cared about you, and was holding you accountable to teach you to be a better person.

When you strike out on your own for the first time, it feels as if it's you against the world. Even though Matt and I had each other and we were building a life together, we still needed a support system for guidance and love. My uncle and my aunt became that for us. When he was diagnosed with esophageal cancer, it was devastating for all of us. He was just fifty-three, so young to be navigating treatments, pain, and exhaustion.

There is a funny story from that time that I want to share. I went to visit my uncle and it was just the two of us, sitting in their big living room. He was on his favorite overstuffed recliner, wearing the Harley Davidson bandana I got him when he lost his hair. His early years were spent in a biker group and he still had a love for motorcycles. At the time I was obsessed with *So You Think You Can Dance* (which is part of the story with my brother Bryce coming soon), and as we watched it Uncle Bert complained. I kept saying, "Well, we can change it." He kept replying, "Nope, nope. Watch it. We're gonna watch it," but he'd go right back to complaining. I think he might have enjoyed grumbling about the show as much as I enjoyed watching it!

Somewhere along the way, he decided to do the Flying Pig Pump and Run – a competition where you lift weights and then run a 5K. Up to that point, I had always said, "If you see me running, you should probably run too because something bad is coming behind me." A lifelong perfectionist who is now "in recovery," I had never enjoyed running because it takes time, consistency, and a lot of struggle and training to find that flow. The "runner's high" doesn't always offset how crappy it feels to be breathing heavy and pounding pavement.

I decided that if my fifty-three-year-old uncle could run a 5k and lift weights while he was battling cancer then I could certainly train and run a 5k. A large group of our family decided the same. Some people ran the 5K or 10K. Others did the full 26.2-mile marathon. At that time, even the 5k seemed like an impossible feat. I spent several months building up my stamina, following a "couch to 5k" program. As I covered those miles, I said many prayers for Uncle Bert and his family.

That was the springboard to my running half-marathons (13.1 miles); full marathons (26.2 miles), and ultra-distances, which is anything over 26.2 miles – usually 50K; 50 miles, and even 100K and 100-milers!

How could I have known that the running seed planted during Uncle Bert's illness would save me and my sanity when I experienced other deaths and life-altering events? It taught me a new way to cope with difficult things in my life. After my brother died, I moved up to the half- marathon and trained and ran and processed my grief. In 2010, I ran the Flying Pig Half- Marathon in honor of Uncle Bert and Bryce. At the beginning of that race, my aunt took a picture over the bridge and there was a huge, gorgeous orb.

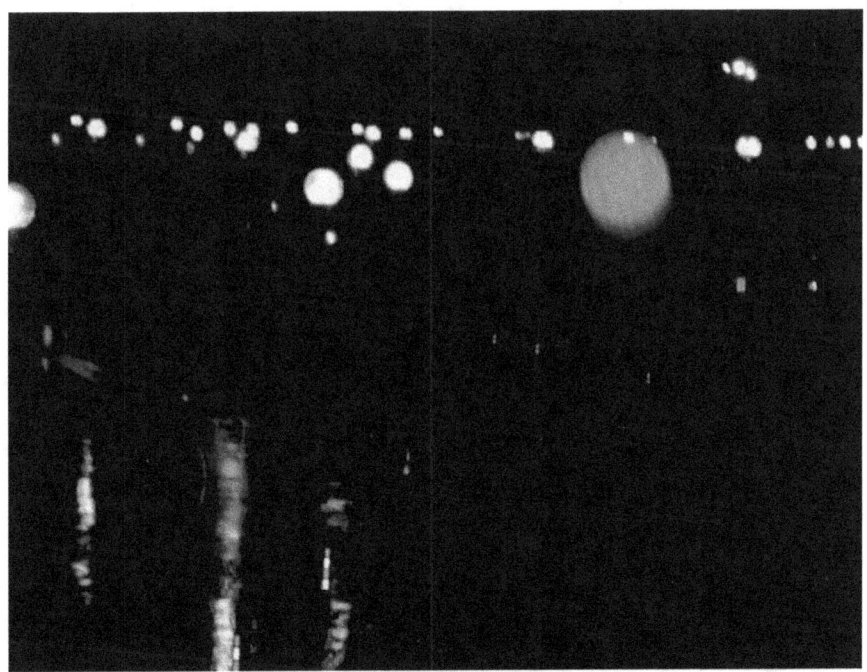

Orb picture from the start of the Flying Pig I ran in honor of
Uncle Bert and Bryce

Orbs, or a round or other shaped light, will show up in photos. They can be spirits that are around but often, they are our loved ones showing us that they are there with us. I have cherished that picture because it's a reminder to call upon my loved ones in Spirit to help me through hard things. Through running I have learned that I can do hard things, physically, but in life as well. With so many difficult things that have happened, I have learned to acknowledge my mental and emotional strength. It helps me in my running so that I can push through longer and harder distances and terrain. The mental toughness has grown from both sides in a beautiful interplay, an exchange of understanding my personal power and my personal growth, so I can believe in myself, that I can do hard things.

And a reminder that so can you.

That is an important lesson that I have taught my own children. They never got to meet Uncle Bert, but his legacy lives on through them, in the power of movement. We often hike over rough terrain. We're climbing hills, and there are rocks, roots, water crossings, heat, and bugs. When they start to complain, I tell them that complaining attracts bears. More appropriately, I will repeat to them, "YOU CAN DO HARD THINGS!" I hope at some point it stops annoying them and instills in them the knowledge that they are very strong, much more so than they give themselves credit for.

I was with my Uncle Burt when he took his last breath, when he transitioned into Spirit and returned to Source. It was a sacred moment that I will always cherish. I would also be with my cousin, Dr. Mike, when he took his last breath, and with my son within me before he ever took his first. These all felt like moments that shifted my very soul. Breath and life force are powerful forces, and when you are with someone as they take their last it is a sacred gift. Not only does it keep us alive, but it can change our physiology if we learn ways to control it. I'll share some of those breathwork practices below.

The Lessons and Blessings

It was an honor to be there as a witness of Uncle Bert's transition and to hold space for his family.

Time passes, and life goes on, but the impact we make on those around us does matter. When he decided to train for that 5k while sick, he inspired me in ways that helped me to improve my life. I've gone on to inspire others and even convinced several people to train for their first races, then pushed them beyond their self-imposed limitations to train for ultras. And that is beautiful. I want to carry that legacy of inspiring others, especially when it comes to doing hard things.

At his burial, several of his cousins brought shovels; this was the start of the family pitching in to bury our dead. The hole was dug with machinery, and the vault was lowered down, but it was our muscle power that filled it back in. There was something visceral that shifted as we worked. We did the same a few months later when my brother died.

Practices from My Uncle Bert

When a tragic or unexpected death occurs, our world goes from being fine one minute to tilting on its axis the next. One of the blessings with cancer is that you do have a lead-up and unfolding of the diagnosis, followed by the battle, when you can say what you need to say and do the things you want to do. Of course, death from any chronic illness feels like many little cuts and then the big wound; you think you're ready to say goodbye, but you never really are.

I still wrestle with the fear that my husband, children, and other people and pets I love dearly will die before I do – and that's okay. The struggle allows me to truly embody and live each day as if it might be my last, but I recognize and work to not stay in that place of fear.

It is never easy to lose someone, but there is a gift in having the ability to prepare for it. It allows an examination of your life, what truly matters, the legacy you want to leave, and an exploration of life and death.

Uncle Bert Did. Not. Give. A. Fuck. what others thought or said about him, in a good way. He would do anything for anybody, but don't mess with one of his own. And I was lucky enough to be one of his own. We have this funny thing in my family where we would add his name to the end of other people's names. Not sure if it was an endearment or an insult, but we'd call people Lizzie Bert, Heather Bert, Alena Bert, and we do to this day! Another legacy to remind us that he's still close by.

As I look to each of the people I have loved and lost, I try to embody what I most admired in them. With Uncle Bert, it was this tenacity and ability to live life on his terms, and I strive for the same.

When Matt and I first got to Lexington, I was about four years into practicing yoga and excited to be in a city with actual studios, rather than having to rely on videos at home. There I was, a white girl from Western PA who showed up for a class to find that it was actually meditation (in the Hindu tradition yoga and meditation are synonymous) to raise the Kundalini energy. Drawing from the teachings from Sahaja yoga and Shri Mataji Nirmala Devi, we focused on breathwork, energy protection, group meditation, and raising our Kundalini energy, then we'd rotate through to help others do the same. We would end with feeling the energy ball between our hands move from warm to cool as our minds, bodies, hearts, and souls sank into a beautiful place of peace and oneness with All That Is. At the time I was still learning about such things and didn't fully understand, but it was powerful.

Kundalini is the feminine form of the Sanskrit adjective meaning "circular" or "coiled." In yoga, the word applies to the life force that lies like a coiled serpent at the base of the spine. It can be sent along the spine to the head through certain postures and exercises.

This release of energy promotes internal balance, awakening, and enlightenment. It can lead to mental clarity and focus. On the other hand, it can also lead to intensification of past traumas, fear, mood swings, and confusion.

It was a whole new world for me. I started raising my Kundalini not knowing it was going to cleanse and clear out everything that was no longer serving me. I also learned about chakras, which is Sanskrit for "disks" or "wheels" and refers to the energy centers in your body. They are spinning energy and each corresponds to certain nerve bundles and major organs. The ideal is for the chakras to stay open and balanced. Today, I incorporate chakra balancing in every session I offer because it is so vital for mental, emotional, physical, and spiritual well-being. At the time, however, I knew nothing about it.

I've since learned other styles of meditation. Meditation has absolutely transformed my mind, my body, my heart, and my soul. As I've integrated meditation into my daily life, I have learned that I am in control of my thoughts, and my feelings and that I can shift and change them. This went even deeper when I learned self-hypnosis as part of my advanced hypnosis training. Now, with a single breath, I can allow a wave of relaxation to flow over me and through me. I can reset, recharge, and rejuvenate my system quickly. I can allow the feelings, but then shift my mindset. It's allowed me to shift and change my relationship with food and my body and truly change those beliefs and patterns on a subconscious level. It has allowed me to access my higher self for healing and to do deeper shadow work, to sleep better and fully embrace and recognize that I am creating my life.

Some of my favorite teachers and practitioners are David Ji, Sharon Salzberg, Archangelology with Kim Caldwell, Lisa A Romano, and

Dr. Janette Freeman; Healing Waves offers Solfeggio tones and binaural beats. These can be found on the app Insight Timer. I use them as I fall asleep, if I wake in the night, as a walking meditation, or if I need a reset beyond what I do for myself in self-hypnosis.

Along with meditation, I learned the value of breathwork and incorporated it into my life. I often teach my clients several breathwork techniques for them to manage and process emotions.

Breathwork influences physiological factors, by stimulating the parasympathetic nervous system to soothe the fight, flight, freeze or fawn response, as well as psychological factors, by shifting thoughts. Deep breathing relaxes our systems, which will increase blood flow, release toxins, and open up lung tissue.

It can create space for the expression and processing of traumas to more easily move toward the surface and be released.

I utilize and teach my clients such things as deep breathing, 4x4 breathing, lion's breath, and I assist them in controlling their breathing as we process past hurts and traumas.

When Uncle Bert was sick, he received Reiki treatments to ease his symptoms and shift energy. I'd heard the term but was not really familiar with it, so this was my introduction to Reiki energy healing.

Reiki, an ancient Buddhist practice, was rediscovered in the mid-1800s and later re-popularized in the 1920s by a Japanese man named Mikao Usui. Reiki is based on the Eastern belief that vital energy flows through the body. "Rei" means universal, and "ki" loosely translates to lifeforce energy. A Reiki practitioner uses gentle touch, or places their hands just above your body, to help guide this energy in a way that promotes balance and healing. While I've never trained in Reiki, I do offer energy healing and balancing as part of my Hypnotic Healing sessions in the way I was shown by Spirit and my Guides.

As I identified the value of movement, I also felt a deeper spiritual benefit from running. I loved *The Book of Joy*, co-authored by the Dalai Lama and Archbishop Desmond Tutu, and found the section about the latter's morning meditation walk (or "constitutional," as he called it) particularly resonant. Tutu never wavered from his routine, even in the midst of the anti-apartheid struggle and death threats he received. He utilized that walk as a way to integrate and listen to the wisdom of the Spirit that often comes through the wisdom of the body. Walking, hiking, running, or any other exercise can be made into a meditative experience. The key to that is to avoid all external distractions like talking, music, or television.

At times I've used movement and music together, or movement while listening to podcasts or audiobooks. And that has its own benefits. But there is true value in using movement as a meditative experience, to listen to the wisdom of the body and the wisdom of the Spirit, in silence.

As I dug further into my Human Design and gene keys, the 24th key in particular struck a chord in relation to the contemplation I'd do as I moved my body. This key is about the shadow of addiction, the gift of invention, and the Siddhi of silence. This addiction can be physical, but it can also be an addiction to our own bullshit or anything else. I've often said that I have an addictive personality, and my "drug of choice" has been food, but there are other things I've taken to an extreme as well.

In reading about the key, I learned that every cycle of addiction has gaps within it, and the only thing that can truly break addictive thinking is silence. This brought about an epiphany: I had fought against silence, real silence, for most of my life, drowning it out with the music or the books or the podcasts or just busy chaos. Now, I am finding that I actually crave silence more and more as time goes on.

Embracing silence is connected to the gift of the 24th gene key, invention. When I allow the silence I can bring new things into the world. It allows new, original thoughts to emerge. From these gaps, I can see things in a new light. One of the best ways to explore these gaps is through contemplation. Contemplation on the mysteries of life and death, on the nature of change and suffering, which can lead to a sudden heightened state of awareness.

I have often used movement – be it running, walking, hiking or biking – in silence as a time to do that very thing, especially when Uncle Bert was battling cancer. When I first started running, I contemplated life and death, going even deeper when my brother died. I noticed that this allowed me to move out of suffering and into greater states of awareness, of deeper insights, of seeing things in a new light and having original thoughts.

The highest expression of this gene key is silence. It's not just about silence around you, but when we stop thinking entirely. This silence descends on you, even though it already lives inside of you. True silence reigns when the mechanisms controlling your awareness moves from your head down into your solar plexus. At that level, you no longer think but *are thought* by life. There is no longer thinking but a knowing and not knowing, simultaneously.

I will continue on this journey of learning to relax because that is the key to finding those magic gaps to experience the truth directly, not through the mind but through my innermost being. This is the great trigger for the enlightenment experience.

Running, hiking, walking, yoga, yoga-meditation, meditation, breathwork, reiki, chakra balancing, silence.

Read over my experiences and notice which most speaks to you.

Take this opportunity to explore and spend some time with each of these practices. You may want to try them on your own or find a practitioner to facilitate the experience. Incorporating practices that connect mind, body, heart, and soul will transform your life just as it has my life and the lives of my clients. In the Hypnotic Healing sessions, we speak to the deep inner self and innate wisdom in the subconscious and can identify the practices that are most beneficial to the mental, emotional, physical, and spiritual well-being.

Me and Uncle Bert

Uncle Bert running the Flying Pig 5K

My first race at the Flying Pig in 2007

CHAPTER 8

MY BROTHER BRYCE

B ryce was born in 1987, when I was six years old. Even at that young age, I helped take care of him; it was as if I was continuing the tradition of my mom's family (she had twelve siblings), where the older kids raised the middle kids and the middle kids raised the younger ones. I felt like a second mom to Bryce, and we had a special relationship. He also drove me crazy because he was so wild.

My son Ian would later exhibit similar frustrating behaviors, and serve as a mirror for me. By that time, I had the awareness to recognize this as an opportunity to heal things that still needed healing. Obviously, at six, seven, and even into my teens, I didn't understand why Bryce's behavior bothered me. However, with my son I've been able to understand triggers and the underlying beliefs that led to that frustration and that anger. More on Ian later.

Regardless, I loved Bryce dearly. He was so much fun and always the bright light that lit up the room. He was the one that made everyone laugh. He was the one that made everyone feel special and loved. That gift carried on throughout his entire life. Given our age difference, as kids we didn't have a lot of overlap with friends or teachers and things like that, but once he "caught up" and we knew more of the same people, I became known as Bryce's sister. This was a good thing. He was the life of the party and gave the best hugs. Unfortunately, like many of us, he didn't know how special and important he was, or how much he positively impacted others.

If you have fallen out of a friendship or family relationship, just let them know that you still love them and still care. Relationships fade and get stronger, they sometimes go away forever, they may be for just a season of your life. But it's still beneficial to reach back and just let them know that they meant something to you on your journey.

Just as watching a loved one slowly fade from a disease, a sudden death assaults the system, just in a different way. There is no preparation. It's a shock. You feel as though the rug has been ripped out from under you. This is what happened that awful day in 2007, just a few months after Uncle Bert died.

Just the day before, I had been riding high as I traveled back to Lexington to meet up with old friends and attend a live showing of *So You Think You Can Dance*. I was so thrilled, so jazzed up and energized about enjoying good food, good company, good music, and, of course, dancing. The very next day, life as I and my family knew it was shattered forever.

It started when, while driving home, I got a call from my dad. Matt was going to meet me partway, he said, but wouldn't tell me what had happened. I assumed at first it was my mom, but then my aunt called, screaming, "Bryce is dead, oh my God, Bryce is dead!" Everything crashed down; I couldn't breathe, then started hyperventilating. What had happened?! When I was told it was suicide, I didn't believe it. I even suspected murder. I would later find out that he had been at my parents' house, not at college as I had originally assumed.

There was a beautiful service at IUP, where Bryce went to college. It was held by the ROTC program he was a part of, and so meaningful because we got to see how well-loved he was. During the two days of viewings the line of people coming to offer their condolences was so long it wrapped around the funeral home, out the door, and all the way across the parking lot. We never got a break, one of the ROTC members was even unwrapping candy and handing it to us. It meant so much that so many people wanted to show up to love and support us through such a devastating time.

After working with people and assisting them in moving through their own traumatic experiences, I recognize how rare this is, that not everyone feels loved and supported through the worst times in their life. But I am always honored to be that person for others.

I wish Bryce had known prior to his death – I do believe he knows it now – just how loved and cherished he was. How much he mattered and the transformational impact he had on those around him.

I think his choice to take his own life was rooted, at least in part, in his belief that he didn't matter. He didn't think he made a difference. He did, just as we all do in our own way, be it for millions of people or just a handful. We all matter and make a difference to someone; thus, we make a difference to the world.

The fact that suicide involves a choice makes it a different kind of death, one that evokes different, conflicting emotions. Sometimes, it can overshadow our love for the person, and for a while it overshadowed my love for my brother. I had so much anger… and so much guilt that would take many years to work through. There I was, a mental health therapist, and my brother had died by suicide. There were no warning signs that I saw or knew about. He was in college and making his own way and becoming his own person. There's so much we can't know as our kids or siblings or other loved ones are starting to make their own way in the world.

I also grappled with fear in the wake of his death. I, as you know, was raised Catholic and went to Catholic school, kindergarten to twelfth grade. One of the things that's taught is that suicide is a mortal sin, which means you go to hell. I do not believe this to be true; however, when you are indoctrinated with beliefs, there's still a small part of you that wonders if they are true. There was even a priest who used him as an example in my cousin's confirmation class.

Bryce was silly, a big goofball who loved to make people laugh. He posed for his senior pictures in the *Star Wars* costumes my mom made him for the midnight showings when the movies came out. Of course, he also had the standard dressed-up pictures, but he had to infuse everything with fun. Well, in the confirmation class the priest somehow wove that in with his suicide, as if my brother was living in a fantasy world. I don't know all the details, nor do I want to, but it was wildly inappropriate; he basically used him as an example of how not to live.

Meanwhile, he had no idea that Bryce was such a special kid and made so many other people feel special.

It also shattered my heart that he died on our other brother's birthday; he even texted him early that morning, "Happy Birthday, brother." He had come home after a night out with friends; then, when my parents went to church, he shot himself in the heart. In the note he left, he said he had made that choice so we could still have a viewing. That was my brother, always thinking of others, even in his most desperate moments.

What he did *not* do was reach out to me – his big sister and second mom, not to mention someone trained in dealing with mental health challenges. This was incredibly hard for me to process. Even now, fifteen years later, the guilt lingers, letting me know I need to further explore my narrative around this. Ultimately, I know it wasn't about me. They are just the emotions I carry.

As we process and find the story of our lives it can help us to process and even rewire our brains around a trauma.

An aspect of grief that isn't always acknowledged is the trauma around the death. It was the pain of knowing my children, who weren't born yet, will never have their Uncle Bryce to look up to and play with. On the other hand, I also know he has my back in everything I'm going through here on Earth – and, more importantly, that he is with Bodhi. Those have been very comforting thoughts.

I am also working to heal my judgment of Bryce's reason for doing what he did. The night before, he had gotten a citation for underage drinking, which he believed destroyed his lifelong dream of becoming a teacher. He was an elementary education major, and with his fun personality and caring for others he certainly would have been an amazing one. I will never know everything that was going through his mind at that time, but he specifically noted in his letter that receiving the citation was not acceptable in the military nor in elementary education.

I think of all the people I know who made mistakes in their youth… because we're supposed to! We're supposed to make mistakes and learn from them, grow from them, and shift and change in the ways that are true to our soul. I know the citation, whether it ended his teaching career or not, was something that he could have overcome, learned from, and helped others through. As I've said, we never know the impact we have, or could have, throughout our lifetimes.

Several of his professors came to the viewing and specifically stated that they would no longer drill into the students the threat of an underage drinking citation ending their career. Indeed, perspectives seemed to have shifted since that time. We are more willing to see the overall person, background and life experiences, rather than just their failings. There is also less shame and secrecy and a greater openness around mistakes. This is a very good thing! When I can be open and vulnerable, it gives others permission to as well. When I can acknowledge that I am always a beautiful work in progress then others realize that is what we're here for, living our best lives while working to learn, grow, and do better.

I have strived to continue his legacy by doing just that: taking everything I experience, learning and growing from it, and then helping others to navigate their own journeys. And, most important, by teaching my kids a mistake is not a life-or-death situation, that everything can be figured out.

Since Bryce's death I have come to understand a lot more about soul contracts and our life paths. I now believe that he came into this world for a purpose, and that at that point, he had fulfilled that purpose. Suicide just happened to be the way he exited. On the other hand, I also think those who die by suicide may have things they must come back to learn. This isn't exclusive to death by suicide, though, as many people fall short on the lessons, they set out to learn in their lifetime and return to try again. Two questions I ask in sessions are, "How did your soul do well?" and "How could your soul have done better?"

Others close to me have also had experiences with suicide. Debi, a dear friend, lost two of her three sons to suicide. They were both veterans and had inner battles they were fighting. In the aftermath, she began to experience suicidal thoughts herself. She has shared with me that on two occasions, what she calls the "spirit of suicide" visited her and encouraged her to take her life. It told her that everything would be better if she died, she'd be happy, she'd be at peace, and more. Whoa, when she told me that I had a visceral, full-body reaction, given the thoughts I've had and the wonderful people I've known who have taken that action. This topic of the "spirit of suicide" was discussed in the documentary "After Death" and was intriguing to learn that others have experienced the same. There is so much pain around suicide, for those left behind as well as for the person who decided to leave this life because they believe negative things about themselves that aren't true, believe others would be better off without them, and/or are in so much physical or emotional pain it doesn't feel possible to go on. I do feel that we have the right to end our pain on our terms, but this is a complicated issue and could be a whole book on its own.

As we move through life, we often think whatever we're going through is going to be the hardest thing ever. Then something else happens and we realize that oh, yeah, no, there are harder things to come, there is more to experience. Losing my brother knocked me to my knees. The moment I found out I had my first panic attack, though certainly not the last. It has also affected me in so many other ways and brought so many lessons about the world and myself.

And still, it did not compare to losing a child. That death fifteen years later rocked me to my core, and rocked almost every belief that I held about myself, about others, and about the world as I knew it.

The Lessons and Blessings From Bryce

Bryce's suicide, while utterly devastating, shifted me in a way that is indescribable. It started me on the path to opening up to my spiritual gifts, my understanding of the Spirit world, and the journey of our souls. Myself, my mom, aunts and others started seeing mediums because it was comforting to have a conversation with my brother in the midst of such tumultuous emotions. We even traveled to Lilydale, New York, which is home to the world's largest Spiritualist community. I had recently reopened my gifts and for the first time felt compelled to share a message with a stranger, with permission of course. Just for fun, we went on several ghost tours at a local college, and I used a pendulum – another first – as a divination tool to communicate with the spirits present. I could feel the entities and hear the stories they were sharing. We had a local medium and a reiki master come to my parents' house for readings and sessions. We had so many people interested in joining us; they came every month for about two years.

Marcy and Sue became my early mentors in the reopening of my spiritual gifts.

Looking back, however, I can also see the synchronicities began even before his death. Matt and I had recently moved back to Pennsylvania and were living in Punxsutawney. I was getting ready to start a new job. I'd spent several years in mental health and worked as a case manager and then as an individual therapist. I would meet the clients each week and we would talk about the same things over and over again. And while they would feel better after talking and using the tools we'd develop in sessions, we never seemed to move beyond the tough things they had faced.

Now, I would be working in community mental health, serving clients deemed "chronically mentally ill," meaning that mental illness has plagued them most of their days. Most weren't able to hold a job or to build meaningful relationships. Many had endured abuse, neglect and other very difficult circumstances. I personally no longer use the term mental illness in my work, but it was the term used by the agency I worked for.

I sat with them each week, held space for them, gave them a place to talk and process their emotions, their experiences. At this time, I was on my own spiritual journey and had come to believe that there had to be more than life on this 3D physical plane.

What I did not believe was the adage, "Life is hard, we suffer, and then we die." It felt like there had to be a better way to process the past hurts we were rehashing every week. I had heard of the benefits of EMDR therapy and wanted to pursue it, but when I found out about hypnosis, specifically for past life regression, my interest was piqued on a whole other level. How could our past lives be contributing to our current life struggles? Could this be a way to heal and understand what people endured and help them move beyond them so they could feel and function at their very best?

This curiosity led to the trip, mentioned earlier, to Sedona for the past-life certification course. It was 2008, the year after Bryce and Uncle Bert died, and those ten days were full of synchronicities and transformative experiences that shifted the course of my life.

Prior to the course I went to visit my Uncle Marty and Aunt Helen, who had retired to Arizona several years before. Marty is my mom's oldest brother and the second oldest in the thirteen-sibling lineup. He is as stubborn and steadfast as they come, he's run multiple 100-milers, including the famous Western States, and the Bataan Death March five times. He also did search-and-rescue for the Grand Canyon and other local parks after his retirement and right up until his heart surgery at eighty-five. My Aunt Helen is incredibly intelligent, level-headed and astute – and the best conversationalist I know. They took me to volunteer at the Zane Grey 50 miler, which introduced me firsthand to the world of ultra events. I had heard about ultras from him, his brothers Bobby and Joe, and my cousin Mike, all of whom had been running ultras for years. I watched Anton Krupica sail into a first-place win and the second-place guy stagger in behind and I was hooked! I've now gone on to run several myself.

When it was time to head to Sedona, several of us taking the course shared a van. We immediately connected and started our deep-dive conversations. I learned that one lady's son had also died on November 11, the same day as Bryce. That was the first synchronicity.

At that time, I didn't know much about Sedona, and I was immediately struck by the unparalleled beauty and strong earth energy that gives you exactly what you need. It is now one of my favorite places on Earth.

Once we got there, I started learning more about the energy vortexes throughout the area. The training was in Angel Valley, so there was much talk about the angels; there was even a special vortex for each of the Archangels. Angels are revered in Catholicism, and I felt myself reconnecting with that beautiful, healing energy.

The past-life regression course completely blew my mind and opened up parts of my inner knowing. These synchronicities played out in real time and others unfolded over time. I have always been a type-A, control freak kind of person, so to think about relaxing and letting my mind go to places that I wasn't in control of was so scary and daunting.

I'll share a story that is both funny and helpful for extremely uptight people who think they will never learn to relax. I was around fourteen years old and had gone to get my nails done for a school dance. The nail tech kept saying, "Just relax your hands, relax your hands. NO, relax your hands!" He kept shaking them, trying to get me to loosen up. That was the first time I had awareness that I had no idea how to relax. I was a perfectionist, a high-achieving ball of tension, so much so that I couldn't even allow myself to enjoy a manicure.

The thought of relaxing and letting go felt almost impossible at the start of the certification course. The other piece that I struggled with was that I am a knower and feeler in the clairs. (Remember to go back to Chapter 4 and determine your strongest clair.) The clairs develop differently for different people; however, I can tell you that when the answers you receive during a regression come through as a knowing or a feeling, it can feel like you're making things up.

Again, I always had that knowing and big feeling part of me, especially around my deceased Aunt Theresa and sister Claire, but at this time I was just beginning to understand my gifts and reopen them.

Before the regression I was expecting to see the scenes like watching a movie, so experiencing the feeling and knowing instead made it difficult to trust. The past life where it all came together, and where I finally let go, was when I was on a boat and could actually feel it rocking. I almost started to panic because I noticed the feeling and was so immersed in it. It absolutely felt real and that I was right there on the boat, rocking back and forth. I even remember coming out of the relaxation thinking, *Whoa, am I still moving?* If you've ever been on a ship or a boat, you know that feeling when you get back to land but it feels like you're still on the water. That was exactly how I felt! It was truly a wild and mind-blowing experience.

That was the moment I understood that I would experience past lives through feeling and knowing, rather than being able to see them like a movie. The more I leaned into and trusted that feeling and that knowing, the more my other senses developed. Sixteen years into offering past life regressions for others, and experiencing them for myself, all of my clairs have blossomed – I can see, I can feel, I can know, I can hear, I can smell. This all happened because I learned to trust myself and the process. That is the biggest thing I reassure my clients of: that this is real and true for them; there is a benefit and a purpose for needing access to this information today. It's really amazing to see people begin to embrace the experience and allow that process to unfold. I've gotten really good at helping even the most nervous people, the people who think it isn't possible for them, to fully relax and allow the experiential session to unfold in a way that is perfect for them.

So many come in nervous or uncertain and leave feeling more healed, that they've gained a greater understanding and clarity that helps them in their relationships. And that helps them shift the way they view or feel about themselves, let go of fears or phobias, or understand why they've been preoccupied with death. It is a truly beautiful and magical experience.

Bryce is now one of my guides and still likes to give me a hard time, in a loving way, from the other side. He is a beacon, reminding me to have more fun and to give things my all.

Bryce's death brought about several Death of Self moments that I have acknowledged over time. The death of wondering if I matter, the death of religious trauma and dogma, and death of holding onto past hurts. Most of these Death of Selfs started here and then have deepened with other deaths and life experiences.

As I mentioned with Grandma Kupchella and, on a deeper level, my brother, there is no such thing as definites, no one issue is black and white. When you grow up with layer upon layer of shame and guilt, it becomes what you believe to be true about yourself. You internalize that you are a bad person, that you are a sinner, that you will go to hell if you do certain things.

I recently had the realization that when anything seemingly bad happens to me I perceive it as a punishment. I had a fear that if I pursued things that made me happy or made my life easier, I would be punished. That somehow if I was more deserving, I'd have enough money or if I was good enough bad things wouldn't happen. Even though consciously I don't believe this, this all lived in my subconscious and I am working to heal it even now.

This showed up when I hired housecleaners. We have three living kids, three cats and three dogs, and busy schedules with work and sports, eating meals and sleeping – you know, life – and it felt impossible to keep up. When your business involves clients there is an up-and-down because their lives affects their attendance at sessions; however, my work had been steady for a few months. Matt was also extremely busy, coaching the boys' Little League baseball teams and playing baseball in a men's league, along with everything else.

The housekeepers came for a consult and I hired them to start asap. That very next week eight clients canceled their appointments and I started spiraling.

"See," I said, "I got too high on the horse, I'm not good enough to hire cleaners," and then I went, "Wait, this is the old story of not being deserving of good things, that I'll be punished for it!"

It took me back a few years, when I'd had Ian. Matt was working and living away and I was drowning. When I hired someone to clean, a comment was made: "Must be nice, I didn't hire someone until I was in my fifties."

Whelp, here it was again, the old story that I didn't deserve help, and the client cancellations was another reinforcement of it. At first, I fell right back in, but I caught myself. There is actually no such thing as deserving. When I realized that I know many shitty people who are living a life of luxury and ease, it shifted something within me. It isn't about being deserving, it is about allowing things to flow and recognizing what is important in my life. I'm choosing to do that and do my best in all areas. This may seem like a story of "privilege," but we can apply it to so many other ways in which I – and many others – sabotage the good things in life.

Practices From Bryce

In my brother's suicide note, he wrote, "I ask that you save your tears. Save them for prayers. Pray for me and, above all, pray for yourselves. I will watch over all of you so that you keep living your lives to the best of your ability."

Below are some of the ways I've tried to do this in his honor.

One of my very favorite memories with my brother was at my cousin's wedding. It was an outdoor reception at a massive log lodge, with tents and tables set up to accommodate the big family. At a certain point, there was karaoke, and the four of us – me, my sister and our two brothers – got up and sang Garth Brooks' "Friends in Low Places."

That leads into the first of three exercises inspired by him.

Engage in inner child healing to heal the pieces and parts that have been hurt in various ways and in different circumstances. This work can allow a more childlike, kid-at-heart, sense of wonderment view of the world. It can allow a healthy and happy internal space when facing life's challenges, no longer triggered by the past.

Inner Child Healing

Journey inward to access, heal, and soothe any parts that need this attention. Oftentimes what we consciously think is bothering us isn't it at all. These techniques, which I utilize in individual and group sessions, allow us to access our subconscious, discover the thoughts and memories that impact our day-to-day functioning, and heal what needs to be healed. The following instructions will allow you to do this for yourself. If you feel you need support in this work, reach out to your therapist or to me for a session.

Place your feet on the ground and begin to notice your breathing getting a little slower, a little deeper, a little more even. Feel your belly soften and thoughts begin to slow. You can do this as you are reading the instructions and the questions. Begin letting go of expectations. Letting go of analyzing the information that comes to you. And now, begin to ask yourself these questions and allow the answers to flow to you, writing your first answer.

> What physical, mental, or emotional pain or problems, or any problematic patterns of behavior or difficult relation-ships do I want to explore today?
>
> Where can I take back power and control in my life?
>
> What does my inner child require for healing and soothing, connecting mind, body, heart, and soul?
>
> Which daily practices will help me to feel and function my very best? For my physical, mental, emotional, and spiritual needs?
>
> What do I need to continue to explore or to heal?

What gifts do I need to embrace and awaken?

What soul-soothing message would my inner child like to offer me?

What I have experienced through many past life regressions is that there is no such thing as hell in the religious sense. I have walked with people through lifetimes where they've done horrific things and they return to the light, just as every other soul I've encountered. That said, there are some souls who choose to not return to the Light and Source. And there are negative energies and entities that remain.

I do think we are meant to be the best versions of ourselves. And that we should take personal responsibility for our actions and for our words. Things that happen in this life are not a punishment for things we've done wrong. There are karmic and energetic consequences to everything we do, for good or for bad, and those lessons will keep presenting themselves until we fully learn them.

This can be done from a place of love and forgiveness and acceptance, rather than fear, condemnation, and shame. And that's what I would like to offer to you today. Where can you shift into those first three and let go of the others?

Bryce questioned his worth when he got that underage drinking citation and believed his dreams of the military and becoming a teacher were gone. What, then, would be true for him?

Who would he be if those things didn't happen? The truth is that he mattered, no matter what. I matter, no matter what; you matter, no matter what. We have inherent value and worth just for being here, just for showing up.

I've helped many people walk that path of healing all those outside influences, letting go of the old stories, even the internal voices that aren't theirs. It might be the voice of a parent or a caregiver or teacher or religious figure or any other number of people of authority throughout your lifetime. It might even be friends or a kid in your class that says something somewhere along the way that your soul or subconscious holds onto and holds you back in some way.

I'm here to give you permission to let those old stories go. To let those voices go that aren't yours. To let go of all the ways that you have sold yourself short. Or when you haven't been true to yourself.

And now, to look at things differently.

Once we breathe into that and accept it to be true that we matter just as we are, then what do we do with that? Where do we go from there?

Place your feet on the ground and begin to notice your breathing getting a little slower, a little deeper, a little more even. Feel your belly soften and thoughts begin to slow. You can do this as you are reading the instructions and the questions. Begin letting go of expectations. Let go of analyzing the information that comes to you. And now begin to ask yourself these questions and allow the answers to flow to you, writing your first answer. And make note below.

Look within yourself, and find your true self. Breathe into your heart of hearts and find what is true for you. Search within for your purpose and understand that you do matter, that you are worthy.

Now, where do you go?

What do you do?

How do you live your life for you?

And then how do you look outside of yourself and do for others?

What would allow you to be the best version of you?

What would that look like?

How will you be living your life once you let go of all outside influences?

What do I know to be true about myself?

What are all the ways I matter?

Bryce and I in 1987.

Laughter

Proverbs 17:22 (NIV):"A cheerful heart is good medicine, but a crushed spirit dries up the bones. Laughter is a gift from God. Laughter is a great way to stay encouraged."

Bryce was a kid at heart. As his Second Lieutenant said in his eulogy, "Who else could master the gridiron and the drama club?" Bryce went all in, in everything he did. He loved football, drama club, and ROTC.

I'll never forget sitting in the audience when he was in a high school play, *Hello Mudduh, Hello Fadduh*. My family and I were already tickled by the humor, but we could not have imagined the next scene: Bryce, wheeling out in an adult-sized baby walker, dressed in a onesie and bonnet. I remember locking eyes with our other brother and just losing it in laughter.

Science has studied and shown the many benefits of laughter.

A laugh lightens your mental load and causes physical changes in your body. Laughter can stimulate your organs. Laughter enhances your intake of oxygen-rich air, stimulates your heart, lungs, and muscles, and increases the endorphins that are released by your brain.

Laughter activates your stress response so it increases and then decreases your heart rate and blood pressure, leaving you with a good, relaxed feeling. Laughter stimulates circulation and aids in muscle relaxation.

Laughter is good for you over the long term. It may improve your immune system. Negative thoughts bring more stress into your system and decrease your immunity. Positive thoughts release feel good hormones that help fight stress and even illnesses.

Laughter can ease pain by causing the body to produce its own natural painkillers.

Laughter can make it easier to cope with difficult situations. It can help you connect with other people, even improve your self-esteem.

In the aftermath of Bodhi's death, I had to really home in on what could make me laugh again. I couldn't laugh, or really even move too suddenly, for several weeks because of the extensive stitching in my perineum. No one wants to split stitches in that area! But once I could safely laugh again, I reached out to the Patdown Crackbabies, the Facebook group of my favorite comedian, Ms. Patricia Williams. You can read her book *Rabbit* to understand the name and history. The group members suggested their favorite episodes and I started relistening. I also started saving funny videos that I could pull up: falling videos are favorites. I'd also reread the running note I'd kept since the kids were little of the funny things they said and did.

What makes you laugh?

Where can you find more laughter in your life? Or find a true smile again?

I often help people find what holds them back from joy and laughter after a death. There can be a lot of factors to work through, but often self-forgiveness is at the core.

Bryce in costume

CHAPTER 9

DEATH THROUGH BIRTH

The birth of each of my children transformed me in different ways.

Issadora came into the world at thirty-five weeks, the first grandchild on both sides. I moved from magical thinking into practical, boots-on-the-ground, figure-it-out mentality. Her birth was very traumatic, but because I didn't know better, in a weird way I felt even more traumatized as I gained more information after the fact. On one hand, it was my fault for not being more informed; on the other I was not told all the risks of Pitocin, of infection, or even of resealing of the sack once the amniotic fluid is ruptured. We took the hospital class only and were not prepared for breastfeeding, especially a preemie, and were not given actual support.

One nurse was so rude and rough, my stress levels would spike when trying to nurse, which, as any mom who has breastfed knows is your worst enemy. Instead of helping me to pump, they pushed formula. As I sat in the NICU leaking bodily fluids, I felt such an overwhelming sense of failure; instead of being encouraged, I was being assured that my instincts were wrong. I wanted to stay and that nurse basically forced me out the door. We sat at dinner down the road, with me crying and wanting to throw up. It is not natural to leave your baby behind and I should have honored my new motherly instincts.

From Day 1, Issadora opened me to motherhood and all the blessings and challenges that it brings. She is so strong in what she believes. Her creative mind is astounding. Now she is fifteen and we have moved into enjoying each other's company. We share a love of diamond art, spooky podcasts, graveyards, and history. We've taken some trips together—one to Salem, two to visit family in California, and we just returned from England for a Glastonbury, Avebury and London adventure. Each of these trips has been so special.

Jacob taught me to explore what was truly important to me. We took natural childbirth education courses after our first traumatic experience and bucked the norm. It taught me to advocate and stand strong. And Matt learned how to best support me and trust our instincts. Jacob's birth allowed us to heal the ways we had been victimized during Issadora's birth and NICU stay. I even had the pleasure of firing that especially nasty nurse during Jacob's NICU stay. We successfully exclusively breastfed for two-and-a-half years, a major feat with a preemie baby. Jacob talks with the Angels and animals; he calls it their spiritual voice. He reminds me to slow down and how to stay centered and grounded. He views the world in such a different way and reminds me to always expand my perspective. After taking the childbirth education classes and after having such a redemptive birth, I went on to get certified and taught childbirth education for several years.

I also believe that, while in utero, Jacob led me to an angel class at the Omega Institute in New York. That's when I met Sunny and Kris Voelker, which changed the trajectory of my life. Kris's music soothes the soul and uplifts the spirit, and Sunny's connection to Source and the Angels has inspired me for over eleven years now. Just being at the Omega Center was so transformative. I met a tarot reader, Marcy, who became a good friend and mentor. I did a shamanic journey that brought pieces of my soul back together after the deaths of College Mike and Bryce, and I met my spirit animal, the snowy owl. I'm still connected with the snowy owl as one of my guides. I experienced craniosacral therapy, during which we communicated with the baby I was carrying, my Jake Jake.

I learned how to protect my energy, to observe, and to no longer absorb other people's energy – vital for any empath. I learned to connect even more with my angels and my guides and to those who are now in Spirit.

Ian, Ian, Ian. He was our planned homebirth and a surprise breech, and yet it was the homebirth of my dreams. As I roared him into this world, more layers of self-doubt fell away and I was so empowered. And then the bottom fell out. I really struggled with postpartum anxiety, depression, and rage, to the point that I once again considered leaving this world. Ian had flipped to breech while I was in labor, which separated my pubic bone. It hurt to walk very badly, stairs were almost impossible due to the pain, anything that amplified that separation sent lightning bolts of pain through my entire body. To make matters worse, a week after the birth, Matt went back to work – and living in his own apartment, two-plus hours away, six days a week. Now I had three kids and two dogs and it was supposed to be back to life as usual. There were days where Ian would nurse and nurse and nurse, and while I had mastered nursing in a baby carrier it still left time when Issadora and Jacob had to fend for themselves.

Running every aspect of a household solo, run a side business and maintain sanity was not great for my wellbeing. One particular day – it was one of those cluster feeding days, nobody had had breakfast – I went downstairs to find Jacob eating raw eggs out of the bowl; thankfully, they were local farm eggs. My old pattern of turning blame towards myself and self-criticism came out in full force.

I felt like I was the worst mother in the world. That nothing I could do was right. On the one hand I wanted to die because I thought the kids would be better off without me, that everyone would be better off without me. But on the other hand, I didn't want to die because I didn't think anybody could do this as good as me. This is the dichotomy of our brains. How can I hold both of those beliefs at the same time? What I actually needed was a death of those expectations and that external pressure that I had placed on myself, that the house had to look a certain way, the kids had to act a certain way, that our food had to be a certain way. Eventually, I rose from those ashes, learning what I needed to care for myself, to be truly whole mentally, emotionally, physically, and spiritually, which is a lifetime work in progress. Ian is all in, all the time and is not swayed by others' opinions or feelings. He is so kind and thoughtful and gives the best hugs. He helps remind me to be better at all of those things too!

I was able to get myself into a much better mental headspace with the help of a naturopath and functional medicine doctor, Dr. Brooke Kalanick. I found her through Sarah Fragoso in one of those beautiful synchronicities – I had followed Sarah when she became famous for her paleo recipes way back in 2004. Now here we were, ten-plus years later, and Sarah had joined forces with this doctor. It has become a massive benefit in that I learned more about brain science and neurotransmitters. I realized there were certain pathways in my body that needed support. There were certain foods and drinks that didn't serve me well because of my body systems. It taught me how to prioritize and understand that food is important, so now how do I meal plan and prep? It taught me to look around my house, and what systems needed to be in place in order to make things as easy and simple as possible. If the kids always forget socks, then have a bin of socks by the front door. Does going down the steps to feed the dogs add an extra five minutes to your morning? Make space upstairs for the dog food. Everything in the house was reevaluated, every system and, most importantly, every belief, was reevaluated. What really mattered?

Taking good care of myself and good care of each other was the priority.

The Blessings and Lessons from Death Through Birth

If talk of wanting to die gives you pause, take that as an opportunity to look back at your past.

Where have you been way too hard on yourself? Where have you held yourself to expectations that were unrealistic, expectations that you could never live up to?

Where have you held expectations of those around you that they could never live up to?

One of my favorite things to say is, "Expectations ruin the day again." And it's true. Having expectations isn't wrong; not expressing them or reacting poorly when they aren't met is the issue.

The thing that has made me the most unhappy throughout my life is caring what others' expectations were of me, of placing unrealistic expectations on myself, and of placing expectations on those around me.

On most days, I can let that go. That said, I find releasing expectations one of the hardest things to do. But now I get to pass those blessings and lessons to my clients. I help them gather the information and put the plans in place that allow them to take good care of themselves, their families, and their careers. I help them improve their mental, emotional, physical, and spiritual well-being. I help them see the practical for themselves, their children or in the way the home functions. This sets them up for success, but also helps them release unnecessary expectations.

There are several Death of Self Lessons I have learned, from when Matt and I decided to start a family, to the first pregnancy, labor and birth (when everything was a learning curve), then actually having our first child, followed by our second and third; a miscarriage; and then the birth, labor and death of our last. There was the death of thinking I'm in control of my kids or their births, death of questioning if I offer anything to this world, and death of perfection. I have also recognized that they are here to teach me just as much as I'm teaching them.

When we have done our own healing work, when we have gone to therapy, when we have read self-help books, when we have really contemplated our past, so that we have worked toward healing our shadows and our hurts. When we can acknowledge our feelings and mistakes. When we are truly living a full life. Only then do the lessons we're here to learn become clear. We can figure out how we want to act or think differently moving forward, or we can see how things worked out for the expansion and growth of our soul. That's when we can really begin to learn what unconditional love truly means.

Many of us grew up with conditional love or the feeling that love had to be earned, that we had to do something to be valuable to be worthy or to be good enough. And, for most of my life, I questioned if I offered anything to this world. If you think about your children, or maybe grandchildren, or a niece, or nephew, I want you to close your eyes, to breathe for a few moments and think about how much love you feel in your heart. If, when you bring them to mind, the smell of their baby soft hair and skin, the easy giggles that they offer, you are unable to notice that feeling of love, it's a good indication that at some point you closed down your heart. You might have put up a wall that, at the time, was needed for safety and self-preservation. But now it's time to heal those hurts and heal your heart so you can feel everything. In the sessions I offer we work on healing those hurts, because when you close off your emotions, you close off the good as well as the bad.

Babies don't have to do anything and we love them. They are not productive and we see them as valuable and worthy. This is so important to remember for yourself!

Just as I have struggled with needing to be productive to feel worthy or deserving or struggling to relax, so do many of my clients. They may even get angry with those who can sit down, do nothing, rest and actually relax.

Our value and worth is inherent and if we come from that place of being enough, then it transforms our entire life. There's nothing that I "should" do. There's nothing that I "have to" do. I, and you, get to make those choices along the way. We get to live our life in the ways that we most want even in a crappy job or in family drama – or worse, tragedy – we still get to choose how we think and act in those moments. When it's done from that place of enoughness it's a much gentler process. We can handle our responsibilities; we can take action to make changes and we can find a place of peace within ourselves.

Now, as I look at control within the framework of my children and of their pregnancy, labor, birth and postpartum, I see there are pieces within our control: doing our own work, engaging in our own healing journey so that we can be the best possible versions of ourselves. Hurt people hurt people; check in to see if you are living in delusion, and let me be the first to tell you that if you're like most people, you are. It comes from a place of wanting to save ourselves and to feel safe, but it's not reality.

I believe that I am meant to take personal responsibility not only for my healing journey, but for educating myself about things like pregnancy, labor and birth. There are things that were in my control. Understanding the vital importance of adequate hydration, of getting enough salt for my blood volume to increase, eating adequate protein, eating adequate vitamin C and other nutrients was vital for the development of my baby and the prevention of complications.

Because I had learned these things it allowed my thirty-four-week-old baby to be very vibrant, and healthy.

I take responsibility to assess what I do have control over and, on the other side, look at what I need to let go of and then where I need to take action. Not just in birth, but in all areas of my life.

There are things that I can do to support the flow of life and things that interrupt that, but control is an illusion.

Even though things happen exactly as they are meant to, there is also the personal responsibilities that I need to take as I navigate my journey here on Earth.

> **"The Buddha taught that we're not actually in control, which is a pretty scary idea, but when you let things be as they are, you will be a much happier, more balanced, compassionate person."**
>
> **~Pema Chodren**

As we look at labor and birth, we see there is so much value in letting go and riding the waves of contractions, of accepting things as they are instead of trying to force things to be a different way. Learning to relax physically, mentally, and emotionally in labor, but really in all of life.

I used to teach childbirth education classes; they were twelve weeks long and focused on teaching people how to relax. Relaxing is not our natural state. Well, it is our natural state, but we have been trained out of it. I would also teach them the different avenues and aspects of physical, mental, and emotional relaxation.

This is now a vital part of my therapy practice because learning to relax is a necessary part of finding that inner peace.

I have examined the belief that I'm in control of my kids and decided that is not a truth or a story I will subscribe to any longer. I'm here to love and guide, but they have their own journey. They will make their own choices along the way. I saw that with each of my children; they had their own journey into this world on a specific day and time. That plan was already in place and then I am the conduit to allow.

I am meant to do my own healing and gain the knowledge that helps them on their journey – whether that is understanding the importance of nutrition and hydration in pregnancy or understanding the importance of movement and massage and chiropractic care to be in the best alignment I can be in. It might be understanding the transition from infant development to child development, understanding breast milk versus formula, baby-led weaning versus pureed foods, on and on as they enter school, teenager-hood and beyond. It is a journey and it is their path, and it is up to me to learn and do my very best for them from a place of love and a place of guidance, not of control and manipulation.

I believe that my children have joined me on this journey to teach me just as much as I'm teaching them. They are closer to God and aren't burdened by the weight of the world yet. One of the questions I get asked most is how we talked to our children about Bodhi's death. I tell them that for us it was an open conversation. As mentioned, Ian cried that he didn't want to die because he didn't remember what heaven was like, and that he'd miss us. I don't believe in making false promises, and because I've experienced untimely deaths I can't say, "Don't worry, I or your dad or you will live a long life," because that may not be true. What I did say was, "Since we don't know what the future holds, we will have as much fun as we can today, we'll live our day to the fullest, and we'll snuggle and enjoy each other's company."

And then I'd ask them some questions and tailor my responses to their needs in that moment. What are you feeling? What do you think happens? What is important for you to do today to feel your best? How would you like to spend time together today?

Practices from Death Through Birth

"There is no normal life that is free of pain. It's the very wrestling with our problems that can be the impetus for our growth."

~Mr. Rogers

As I navigated each of my children's pregnancies, labor, birth, and parenting each of them, there were several blessings and lessons that stood out to me. The biggest of all was that I can push my limits beyond what I ever thought possible. I can do things that I never imagined doing. I am now willing to fail in the pursuit of my dreams, physical goals, career goals, and so much more.

I have progressed from 5Ks to half marathons, to marathons, and to ultra distances. I even ran sixty-nine miles for my thirty-ninth birthday, running for twenty hours and thirty-two minutes and convincing a cousin and a friend to do it with me. Years ago when I started running I never imagined that I would ever make it to ultra distances when a 5k seemed nearly impossible.

At the age of thirty-eight I took up jujitsu. It is a sport of failure. As you tap (which signals to your opponent that you want to quit), you learn from your mistakes. You learn the weaknesses in your game and, most importantly, you learn where to strive for improvement. This is the same desire I have for my life.

There have been many times in my life that I've quit. I quit the dream of medical school because I was afraid I wasn't smart enough. I even quit bowling in grade school because I couldn't immediately throw strikes.

I gained a lot of weight during my pregnancies and had to come back from that – working to regain strength and endurance, gain muscle and lose the fat four times now. I donated a kidney to my dad in October of 2023 and have had to build back from major abdominal surgery and my body adjusting to one kidney.

After Bodhi's death I fell into a very bad place around my body and with food, and even alcohol. I was so frustrated that I had gone through a pregnancy at age forty that destroyed my body, that I had gained a lot of weight and sustained a massive birth injury, and I had no baby to show for it. I returned too often to that place of self-hatred and was eventually diagnosed with Lyme and Bartonella infections.

I noticed heart issues, recovery issues, and other internal system issues. But as that unfolded, I recognized yet again that it was a chance to either quit on myself or to work to heal – learning, understanding, and accepting my body on an even deeper level. On what foods do and don't work, what supplements are needed, on how important sleep is, as are my mental well-being and physical needs.

> Ask yourself these questions too.
>
> What does your body need from you?
>
> What foods or drinks are needed or should be avoided?
>
> Are there any supplements to enhance my well-being?
>
> What do I need to be mentally and emotionally my best?
>
> How is my sleep?
>
> Am I resting enough?

One of my very favorite pieces of my life is hiking with my kids and dogs. It's always an adventure, something to whine about and something to celebrate. The kids remind me to slow down and admire nature and the simple things in life. When Jacob was a toddler, we started with a goal of hiking once a week all summer. He'd spend some time in the baby carrier and walking some on his own. We have continued every summer since. Each kid then transitioned to carrying their own pack with water and snacks. They have hiked some big trails and sometimes we only make it a mile or two. They love water crossings and waterfalls the most, but can find anything to get excited about! We added paddleboarding and kayaking during the pandemic summer. I often remind them they can do hard things when the going gets tough.

Nature was a way for me to find an even better version of myself as I hiked or ran through it.

Nature is so soothing, so healing, and has been a very necessary part of my life and grief journey. Even as a young kid I gathered rocks and sticks and made "potions." And now my kids love to gather the same things.

In the midst of my grief, I would go out in nature for races or training runs or to walk and take pictures. I focused on finding beauty all around and noticing the elements, as each benefits me in different ways. I'm a fire sign, so I find the water very soothing and cleansing. Earth grounds and balances me and calms me down. Air invigorates me and brushes away pent-up energy, anxiety, or any other emotions. Fire lights me up in that figurative sense; it inspires me, it fuels my creativity, it helps me to release what no longer serves me. The winter after Bodhi died, we started doing fires. We'd put on our snowsuits, Matt would cook on the outdoor oven, and we'd sit around the fire and play in the snow.

I encourage you to get out in nature and connect in the ways that work best for you. It might be planting a garden or having a plant in the house. It might be having a fire outside or lighting a candle. It might be listening to the wind through windchimes or feeling it blowing over your skin outside. It might be putting toes in a stream or submerging completely in a shower or bath.

Not only does actual nature help and soothe me, but going to my special sacred place in my mind is very powerful. This is a technique I learned from my hypnosis teacher Mary Elizabeth Raines. It is a technique I teach my clients as well. It's a place to go to feel good, to look good, to make any changes, to release what no longer serves me, and/or to connect on a deeper level with my spirit team. This can be a real place or imaginary or a compilation and it doesn't need to be logical; this is a special place in whatever form it takes.

I have two versions that incorporate all the senses. One is in the dry, red rocks of Sedona in the shaman's cave. When I go there, I feel that connection to the universal truth and wisdom and the connection to the collective consciousness. The other is a waterfall with a natural pool below it with ancient rocks and moss surrounding it. Here I can release what no longer serves me, I can make the changes that I want to make, and gain clarity, insight, and wisdom to understand situations better and to do the healing that I need to do.

My love of nature was reinvigorated after I had kids because we could get away from the busyness, the chaos and the never ending to do list. As we hike these adventures teach us so much about ourselves.

It showed us that we can do hard things. It showed us how to slow down so that we can see the beauty in the simple. The water droplets on a leaf or the perfect combination of rocks and moss and trees. Or the rushing water or just a simple creek or water crossing. Finding a "good" stick, which for the boys were ones that could be guns or rockets, was key, as were the perfect, special rocks, purple mushrooms, seeing animals and birds, finding feathers and bones, and so much more.

The connection to nature may be with the moon and using her cycles to bring that sacredness and intention into day-to-day life. Or it might be looking at the sunrises or sunsets or noticing the sun rays shining through the clouds. It might be driving along and noticing the flowers blooming or the seasons changing. It might be the nature smells, the smell of the fall leaves or the flowers warmed by the sun in the summer. It might be seeing the baby deer in the spring or the sparkling glittery snow in the winter. Nature is different everywhere, but there is beauty wherever you live.

As I move through life, I have recognized how very important it is to explore the shadow aspects of myself. I especially recognized this once I had kids. It was like they were a mirror to show me all the ways I needed to heal and do better.

In shadow work we look at the darkest parts of ourselves, where they've come from and what we need to know about ourselves and about the world. This is to learn to not allow it to overtake us and how to balance it out.

Our shadows are the dark emotions or behaviors that are often pushed down but tend to creep out in times of stress or vulnerability. I say that shadows can be like a beach ball – the harder and further it is pushed down the more it will explode out of the water, usually at inopportune times.

Emotions can show us what areas of life need a change. What upsets me in others is often something I don't like about myself.

In the depths of pushing away my shadows I have learned that I can see my shadows and honor them. I can make choices and, in some circumstances, use them for my and others highest and greatest good.

In my shadow work with clients, we identify them and then look to shift it into a gift. When we embrace all aspects of ourselves, we can truly heal.

I am very kind and compassionate, but I can also be a dick. I have turned this into an ability to advocate for my clients and to stand up for those who may not be able to for themselves.

I can be a know-it-all, I can be bossy, I can be controlling, I can be per-fectionistic. I have used all of these traits to work hard and strive to be my very best. I have used it to build my business, take care of my kids, animals, and house while my husband lived and worked away. While I have learned to tame the dark side of those traits, I still use them to find what success means to me.

As mentioned, I am now moving them into understanding astrology, Human Design, and my gene keys – essentially what I'm here in this life to learn and experience.

Shadow Work Journal Questions

Place your feet on the ground and begin to notice your breathing getting a little slower, a little deeper, a little more even. Feel your belly soften and thoughts begin to slow. You can do this as you are reading the instructions and the questions. Begin letting go of expectations. Letting go of analyzing the information that comes to you. And now begin to ask yourself these questions and allow the answers to flow to you, writing down your answers.

What patterns have you noticed that have repeated through-out your lifetime?

What fear consumes me?

What angers me about others? About myself?

What parts of myself have I tried to push down throughout my life?

What are the stories I've created from these feelings?

How can I shift the story?

How can I transform my shadow into a gift?

Paddleboarding on Cloe Lake

At the top of the Thousand Steps trail, there was so much whining on this one!

Kids and Puppies!

We love to hike barefoot

One of my all-time favorite hiking pictures. I loved those days of hiking while babywearing—such special memories that I truly miss!

CHAPTER 10

MY COUSIN, DR. MIKE

In the winter my parents used to go to St. Maarten. My kids and I visited them there several times and found the scenery, the ocean, and the people so beautiful. On our last trip to the island we were joined by my cousin through marriage, Dr. Mike. I was excited because he was someone I'd always looked up to. When I was pursuing medical school, he mentored me and got me an internship in a pathology department. He had a deep faith and loved his family more than anything.

As mentioned, my mom came from such a large family that the ages of my relatives are really spread out. The oldest siblings were out of the house, working jobs, and getting married before the younger ones were even born, so I have some cousins in their fifties, sixties, and even now into their 70s. My oldest cousin is older than my youngest aunt.

Mike married a daughter of my oldest aunt. My mom and her niece were having children around the same time. My younger brother and Mom's niece's oldest were the same age and then down the line. Their daughter was the same age as my youngest brother and then their youngest was the same age as my youngest sister. They also lived nearby, so my siblings and I were close to them growing up.

Dr. Mike called himself a "country doctor" because he had practiced medicine in small coal mining towns similar to the one he had grown up in. He'd go on to become the Chief Medical Officer of the closest large hospital, but was always a country boy at heart. He retired shortly before his death, and then only because of his health issues.

There were many things I admired about him. Some of my most vivid memories were attending folk mass on Saturday nights in our small town, and he would lead the music with his guitar, his voice, and his presence. His presence was one of intelligence, of faith and of loyalty. I noticed within him a desire and need to always do better for the community and be a better person. Even more important to him was helping people feel better, and he did that through his work as a small town, country doctor, where your primary care physician is your everything.

Making the community a better place was also very important to him. He was in the process of raising money to erect a chapel at the cemetery. The local Catholic Church had closed, the stained-glass windows sold off, and the building sold. Thanks to synchronistic events and his tenacity, he managed to track down the original stained-glass windows that were in the church before it closed.

He was instrumental in cleaning up the waterways that had been polluted by acid mine drainage. In the last several years there have been fishing derbies held in the Blacklick River, and even though locals still call it the Sulphur Crick it is now cleaner and supporting fish and wildlife again.

Mike was also an ultra-runner, as were my uncles, Joe, Bobby, and Marty. In my younger years that was so mind-blowing to me. Mike ran the Laurel Highlands 70-miler, the JFK and Bull Run 50-milers, the Vermont and Western States 100-milers, and many others.

God bless his wife for running the household and managing the kids while he pursued being a doctor, which took a lot of time, and his running, which took even more.

He, along with my Grandpa Kupchella and others from the town, turned the old railroad tracks into a Rails to Trails, thanks to a bill passed in 1976 and the Rails to Trails Conservancy that formed in 1986. Our local trail is called the Ghost Town Trail as it snakes through many rural areas that once had mining or logging towns, now long abandoned. Every Sunday he would get out there and run.

It was fitting that the last chance I got to spend time with Mike was on St. Maarten, one of my favorite places on Earth and definitely one of his. He would say that he could feel the pain and tension leaving his body as the airplane started to descend to the island's tiny, very dangerous airport.

The sun is always shining, and if it happens to rain it passes quickly and right back to beautiful sunshine. The temperature is always right around eighty. The water is that gorgeous turquoise Caribbean blue. The place where we stayed in St Maarten had beautiful white sandy beaches and a protected cove with perfect waves.

When Mike arrived, we had already been there for a few days – walking off the porch and onto the beach, playing in the water and sand all day and heading to the pool and hot tub in the evening. We'd even gone all the way to the tippy-top point of Fort Amsterdam to look out at the waves crashing and the pelicans nesting, admiring the different plants, including the aloe plants the local women used to massage beachgoers. Truly paradise.

On his second day there we went to the Parrotville bird sanctuary, one of my favorite places on the island. The original had been destroyed during Hurricanes Irma and Maria. The owner had saved all two hundred birds, taking them to the barn on his property when those massive storms hit and wreaked havoc on St. Maarten and other nearby islands. The damage was devastating, but he had built it back even bigger and even better.

Dr. Mike also loved this bird farm. He spent the whole time trying to catch pictures of the grouse that hid under the bushes and the local plants that supported the birds inside the sanctuary. We got our cups of food that the birds love to land on and walked around. I noticed him sitting at different points on the benches scattered around, sitting in front of the water feature listening to the waterfall cascading down and watching the little birds land and get a drink and wash themselves in the water. Then he'd get back up and meander along the gravel trails, looking for the grouse.

All was well and we were all settling into a lovely vacation. The next day we were celebrating my mom's birthday and went to dinner. Mike said he wasn't feeling good and that he'd eat dinner in his room. We didn't think anything of it; he didn't indicate that it was anything serious.

After dinner we made our way to bed. My kids and I were sharing the king room, with a big bed for me and the two boys and a cot for my daughter. My mom and dad were using the pullout couch in the living room and kitchen area. There was a whole separate room for Dr Mike with a kitchenette and a bathroom so he could be completely separate and have his own vacation experience, and then come over and use the big kitchen and hang out when he wanted.

Around two a.m. my mom came in, shook me awake, and said that Dr. Mike was in trouble. I was in one of those deep sleeps from a long day of sun and sand and water. I jolted awake, jumped out of bed with my heart racing, mouth filling with heat and saliva, fear, and panic setting in. Feeling the cold tile under my feet was a shock as I made my way quickly across the rooms. As we hurried she was explaining that he had yelled for my dad, told him he was having trouble breathing, and had already called for the ambulance.

In the meantime, my dad and I went to see if we could help him. Mike wanted to stand up and Dad was trying to help him as the ambulance attendants arrived and took over. As they were attempting to treat him, he collapsed into their arms.

I could see, feel, and sense his soul leave his body and asked the Angels to be with him and all of us as we navigated this devastating situation.

I felt the cold tile under my feet again and felt a wave of sadness wash through me. But also, a great peace as I knew his angels and his dad were meeting him as he returned to the arms of Jesus, who he had spent a lifetime celebrating through mass and his music.

I then immediately dropped into practical mode; the coroner was called, the upper management had already been called and had arrived, the ambulance staff began to ask us questions and the coroner arrived to ask even more. In the meantime, I went into the huge bathroom and sat on the edge of the tub and tried calling his wife; it was two a.m. in the States and the phone just rang and rang and rang and rang. Next, I called his oldest son, and with a quavering voice and holding back my tears because I knew their grief would be exponentially worse than mine, I told him that his dad had died. Giving someone you grew up with some of the worst news of their life, and in such a sudden and unexpected way, shifts your soul.

I had to tell him several times before it fully sank in and asked him to go to his mom and tell her. Shortly after his other son called and said he just needed to hear it straight from my mouth. My heart broke even more as realization sank in. Mike had only been in his sixties, still so young. The grandbabies he adored wouldn't get to know him in the way I had, the way I was blessed by his presence, now only his memory.

But I didn't have time to wallow or sink into those feelings. Unlike the States, the coroner in St. Maarten is a medical doctor and she had a lot of questions for us. We answered as best we could. Meanwhile, I was fearing that we would somehow be held responsible or get in some kind of trouble, and I worried for my kids. Thankfully, they'd slept through the entire ordeal, though of course we had to tell them the next morning what had happened. They adored Dr. Mike and were very sad to hear the news.

We wanted to keep things as normal as possible for them, but stepping out into that glaring sun the next morning was surreal. It was like everything that had happened the night before was just a nightmare. The worst kind of nightmare of things being fine one moment and not fine the next.

Dr. Mike at the bird sanctuary in St. Maarten

Me, My Dad, Dr. Mike and Annie.

The Blessings and Lessons of Dr. Mike

Everyone's journey around the loss, even of the same person, is very different.

I felt blessed that I got to be with Mike in his final days and in his favorite place on Earth. It is indeed a sacred thing to watch somebody take their last breath and be greeted by the Angels and loved ones that went before.

I learned so much from him as to the kind of person that I want to be to my family and to my community. But I also thought I would follow in his footsteps and become a doctor. His guidance during that time and especially the pathology internship he facilitated provided priceless life experience. It was exciting, thrilling, and challenging. It pushed me out of my comfort zone to interact with doctors and lab techs and autopsy technicians, the local coroner, and even the local and state police. And while I didn't go to medical school, the biology and chemistry degrees provided a foundation that helped me as a medical social worker. It encourages me to stay abreast of the research in brain science. It taught me to critically think and analyze what I experience, even in the mystical sides of life.

To have to call his family in the States and give them this terrible news was difficult, but holding space for people as they navigate these difficult moments is an important part of my work. Not fixing or saving, but staying grounded, present, and compassionate is my role and was in those moments for his family too. His long-term service to the community as a small-town doctor, his deep faith, and love of his family continue to inspire me to serve, honor my own faith, and put my family first.

Practices from Dr. Mike

As I mentioned, my brother didn't feel and know how important he was to so many. His death allowed me the Death of Self of wondering if people actually care, if I actually matter.

Dr. Mike's death solidified the lessons I had begun learning after losing Bryce. As I sat with the grief around Mike's loss, with the shock waves rippling through the family and the community, I saw again just how much difference one person could make. As I thought about all the ways he blessed my life, I wished I had told him how thankful I was. But I do trust that he knows it now.

Pause to think, and maybe even journal, about the people who have mattered to you. What would you like to say to them? Remember that we can communicate on a soul-to-soul level, even if they have died. We can communicate with them and we can let them know what we think, what we feel, and that they matter to us.

In one type of session I offer, I help facilitate that conversation with those in Spirit. We work so you can feel them, hear them, see them and experience them. We open that door so that you can begin to see the signs, symbols and synchronicities from them or other Spirit Team members.

Another option is to write a letter that you keep or that you can choose to burn and transmute that energy. Sometimes these relationships were complicated in life and are still complicated in death. And it's okay if it's complicated. There is research supporting the power of a gratitude letter and its benefit for the sender and receiver, so let's dive into it.

> Get quiet, close your eyes, take a few deep breaths and sink into your heart space.
>
> Write out all the ways they helped you.
>
> How they impacted your life in a positive way.
>
> What they truly meant to you.

Evaluate the impact you want to make on the world. Get quiet, close your eyes, take a few deep breaths, and call upon a special loved one in Spirit to help you access the best parts of yourself.

If any of these feel like a struggle, breathe gently into it and imagine that I am sitting with you and infusing you with the ability to see all the amazingness I see in you.

> What are my gifts?
>
> What are the things I'm really good at?
>
> What do people compliment me on or thank me for?
>
> What am I passionate about?
>
> What causes are close to my heart?
>
> What are all the good and unique things about me?

We can offer gratitude for the people that mean the most to us and we can offer gratitude for all of the blessings, large and small, in our life. Developing a gratitude practice is beneficial on many levels. Harvard Health reports that "Gratitude is strongly and consistently associated with greater happiness and helps people feel more positive emotions, relish good experiences, improve their health, deal with adversity, and build strong relationships."[8]

An important aspect of a gratitude practice is really feeling it deep within. I would encourage you to take time each day to write out and feel 3 to 10 gratitudes. It can be simple things like a flower blooming or big things like a new job opportunity; it can be gratitude for things in your past or an upcoming trip or anything that speaks to your soul.

This is a practice that contributes to well-being, just as offering gratitude to those who have meant a lot to us does too.

---

[8] Harvard Health Publishing. Aug 14, 2021. "Giving Thanks Can Make You Happier." https://www.health.harvard.edu/healthbeat/giving-thanks-can-make-you-happier

CHAPTER 11

MY ANIMALS' DEATHS AND MY SOUL DOGS, CAMILLE, AND SALVATORE

I can't write a book on grief without talking about my animals. Animal deaths can be some of the hardest deaths we face.

Oftentimes, other humans have failed my clients over and over again, causing so much pain and so much hurt. Their animals are the ones that bring them peace and comfort and unconditional love.

As I've mentioned earlier, growing up I often felt misunderstood and that I was a bother.

I had a dog, Camille, who was born just a few months before I was. Dad's purebred springer spaniel Nicole had puppies in May, and he knew I was coming in July so he decided to keep one of them. Camille was a mutt, medium to large-sized, and had curly hair with a mix of browns.

Camille was one of those soulmate dogs. She was always there when I most needed her. When I went outside to cry, she would come to me; she had a peaceful, calming presence as I played. I am lucky enough to have another soulmate right now, in my dog Salvatore, because he helped me so much when Bodhi died and in my kidney donation recovery.

Because Camille was with me from infancy on, she was so gentle not only with me but with the other kids who came to the house – cousins, friends, and the like. We lived in the middle of the woods with only one neighbor within sight. Other than my siblings – one brother close in age, the other six years younger than me, and a sister eleven years younger – there were no other kids around regularly, Camille became my best friend. We'd check on the chickens together. She'd watch as I swung grapevines. I'd play on the swing set and she would always be close by. She had several litters of puppies throughout my childhood. My dad would get her a baby pool with blankets ready and she would have cute spaniel and boxer puppies. I can still picture their squishy little faces and remember she was such a good mom until the puppies went to a new home.

She was my solid companion for sixteen years until she got sick. It was devastating, but it was so special to have her as my soul dog for so long, a true gift.

When I was in high school, my grandparents took us to West Virginia each winter as our Christmas gift. We would sled and ice skate and play games. There was no TV and it was the time before the distractions of the internet and cell phones.

My grandpa would bring the newspaper from home to read while we were gone. In a Divine synchronicity, as I would have never read the newspaper at home, I was looking in the classifieds and found an advertisement for puppies. They were close to our house, and I successfully convinced Dad to take me to see them. There was one with big brown eyes, huge paws, and I knew he was mine. Throughout my life I've had weird obsessions and interests. At that time, I was very into

WWE Wrestling. We would get the wrestling pay-per-views and have big parties in the living room. My favorite wrestler was Buff Bagwell and so I named this new puppy Buff. He did get huge to match those big paws! During hunting season, we put orange on him because he looked like a white-tailed deer going through the woods.

He was only a few years old when his stomach flipped. He had a big barrel chest and if they run after they eat, their stomach can flip. That was something I didn't know anything about at the time. The vet told us they could do surgery; the problem was that once the stomach flips it will usually flip again so we had to say goodbye to another animal.

In 2004 I began working toward my Master of Social Work at the University of Kentucky in Lexington. Matt and I, who had married that Labor Day weekend, were living in an apartment but looking for a house. I was looking on Petfinder and found this beautiful Mastiff mix at a foster in Cincinnati. The moment we met her, we fell in love. We named her Mia, but often called her by her nickname, Pupper. A good friend, Cori, agreed to take her until we closed on the house. Pupper's other half was Chow, and though she was beautiful and loyal she didn't like anybody but us – with one exception. She became good buddies with Cori's dog so we humans would take turns hosting playdates.

About a year later we went to the Lexington Humane Society and found this little Jack Russell Beagle mix that we named Bud, but he became Puppy. When I went to pick him up, one volunteer said, "Ohh-hhh, you're taking himmmmm," while another volunteer very quickly elbowed her. I should have known he'd be a handful! Puppy was full of energy up until the day that he got sick at age fourteen. He would train with me for my half and full marathons. We'd come back with me heaving and exhausted and him racing around as if he hadn't run at all!

The dogs were older by the time we had children. Puppy took to them, but Pupper was grouchy so we couldn't let the kids play with her. Mia got progressively slower and had more and more difficulty walking so we made the decision to end her suffering. It was the first time I had to make the call and it was so difficult. A year later, out of nowhere, Puppy got sick and he was suffering so bad I made the call at the vet without the kids saying goodbye. They still tell me that made them very sad, but I couldn't see him suffer anymore. We've talked about their feelings and allowed it all to come up. Pushing things down or shooing them away doesn't allow healing and we will use all tools to process grief, for humans and animals alike.

It especially hit my daughter hard. We were set up at a metaphysical expo, she for her art and me for my past life and hypnosis sessions. We always like to walk around and see and meet the other vendors and what they are offering. I was so drawn to a medium and animal communicator named Joan that I signed up for a session. We met several of my loved ones, but then she said I needed to get my daughter because Puppy was coming through for her. As he offered her his messages through Joan, I witnessed the emotion flow and a peace settle over her. I have brought into my sessions the permission for people to say what they need to say and also to receive the messages they most need – sometimes from humans, sometimes from animals, always powerful and transformative.

We only lasted a week before we started searching for a new dog, even though I had vowed we'd wait longer. When I stumbled across an adorable beagle boxer mix named Angelo it seemed like another Divine sign; little did we know we'd end up with an extra special dog too. Angelo has always been one of my favorite names and then when I met my husband it was his grandpa's name. He died shortly before Ian was born, so we gave him Angelo as his middle name. Ian is Scottish for John, which is for both of his grandpas and great-grandpa too. When we went to meet Angelo, my husband noticed this super-sad puppy all alone that was already about six months old. He had the sweetest face and saddest eyes and he said we just have to get him!

"Two dogs?!?!" I exclaimed, "Sounds good to me!"

We named him Salvatore and he is another soul dog. Even people who don't like dogs love him. Everyone wants to take him home. He was my comfort animal when Bodhi died and I was stuck in bed recuperating, and he continues to be a huge source of comfort. He helped me through my kidney donation recovery too. We went on to add two black kittens that a friend rescued. Those two have helped the other kids heal in the way only animals can. And we added a Great Pyrenees-English Shepherd; she is busy herding all of us humans and the other animals and is pure joy!

I believe that each animal is divinely guided to us when we most need them.

The Blessing and Lessons from the Animal Friends

There are so many lessons that we can learn from animals – be they on our Spirit Team, our pets, and Guides or what some cultures call Spirit Animals. The biggest lessons I've learned from my animals is the power of the soul connection and the power they have to heal and soothe us. I've even witnessed animals who have come along from a past life.

They have shown me that if I listen to my inner wisdom and to that divine guidance that as we lose one pet it may lead us to our next. The gifts and love they've given us go beyond the physical and live in the heart. Because there is no verbal communication, they teach us how to be in our heart space.

I struggle with intellectualizing my feelings, and so many of the clients I see have learned to do the same. They have done this for safety, for self-preservation, or because they just didn't understand or know how to process and actually feel feelings. Animals can help us to heal those emotions.

I love noticing the signs and symbols and synchronicities from my pets, as well as animals in the wild, and communing with the animals that show up in our life. I first feel into the wisdom and messages that they are bringing to me using my intuition, and then oftentimes dive deeper and look up their spiritual meaning. I have most of Ted Andrews' books and they are my go-to resource on animal wisdom.

As mentioned, while at Omega for the Angel class, I connected with a snowy owl. We went on a shamanic journey together to bring back the pieces of my soul that had been splintered when College Mike and Bryce died. I had a beautiful journey through nature on the back of that owl, and at the end the owl turned and merged into me and has become a guiding presence since.

I have sought out the wisdom of animal communicators – people who connect with the animals around us, be it our current pets, deceased pets, or animal guides. While it's wonderful to access outside validation, it is also wonderful to learn to connect on our own. I especially love helping people connect to their pets that have crossed over into Spirit or their animal guides and other animal friends.

Another lesson the animal realm can offer us is there is no such thing as value or worth. We see our animals as valuable and worthy just as they are; we actually have to do for them. And yet, we judge ourselves harshly thinking that we have to do more and more. That we have to somehow earn our value and worth. Take a few moments to pause after reading through this section. Slow down and get in touch with your heart space, that place where you connect with your pet or a favorite animal – be it one you've seen in the wild, on a farm, or even at a zoo. Settle into that heart space. Breathe deeply and allow that connection to flow. Now, begin to notice the messages that your special animal wants to offer you. Allow the animal to share with you your inherent value and worth.

Another common trial that my clients face is loneliness. During a session with one of my extra special clients, we received the message that there is a purpose to loneliness. In the loneliness they had the space to expand their soul because they read and learned and explored more than they would if their calendar was jam packed with frivolous activities and were overrun with responsibilities.

Everyone feels lonely at one time or another; however, if you have felt that loneliness is a hardship and another hurt in your life, I encourage you to explore that. I encourage you to shift your perspective of loneliness, for example: How can this allow me to expand? How can this allow my soul to grow? How and where can I begin to find the people who feed my soul?

Shortly after that session I read this excerpt from Pema Chodron's book, *When Things Fall Apart: Heart Advice for Difficult Times,* and it really cemented the message that came through.

> When we can rest in the middle, we begin to have a non-threatening relationship with loneliness, a relaxing and cooling loneliness that completely turns our usual fearful patterns upside down. Usually, we regard loneliness as an enemy. Heartache is not something we choose to invite in. It's restless and pregnant and hot with the desire to escape and find something or someone to keep us company. When we can rest in the middle, we begin to have a nonthreatening relationship with loneliness, a relaxing and cooling loneliness that completely turns our usual fearful patterns upside down. There are six ways of describing this kind of cool loneliness. They are: less desire, contentment, avoiding unnecessary activity, complete discipline, not wandering in the world of desire, and not seeking security from one's discursive thoughts.

We can look to our animals for an even greater understanding of this. They don't second-guess. They don't doubt; they simply acknowledge and allow things as they are. Where can I, and where can you, accept things a little more deeply? The animals have allowed me to see the simple joys and pleasures and I encourage you to allow that for yourself.

Think of how happy a dog is every single time their owner comes home. They may have just walked out the front door and quickly returned because they forgot something, and the dog will be just as happy to see them again. Look for those simple joys each day. Doing that allows movement from loneliness and into expansion.

Practices from the Animal Friends

Here is an opportunity to meet and connect with an animal friend.

Place your feet on the ground and begin to notice your breathing getting a little slower, a little deeper, a little more even. Feel your belly soften and thoughts begin to slow. You can do this as you are reading the instructions and the questions. Begin to let go of expectations. Let go of analyzing the information that comes to you.

In your imagination, notice yourself on a path in a sacred, healing forest. (If it's more comfortable, you can create your own scene using all your senses. There is no right or wrong way.) Feel the warmth of the sun shining through the trees, see the shades of green in the leaves and moss and pines, smell the deep earthy smell of the woods, brush your hand along the rough bark. As you make your way to a clearing in the trees, you feel the connection growing. You can invite an animal friend, an animal guide, or a deceased pet, into this space with you.

And then you can move through all of your senses.

Notice how you see them; it could be a full form or a shape or a color.

How do you hear them? It could be their animal sound or another sound.

How do you smell them?

What tastes can remind you of them?

How do you feel them? A physical sensation? A tingling, the pressure of a hug, or something else?

What emotions do you feel when they are near?

And now ask them what message they would like to give you.

Make note below of what you experienced.

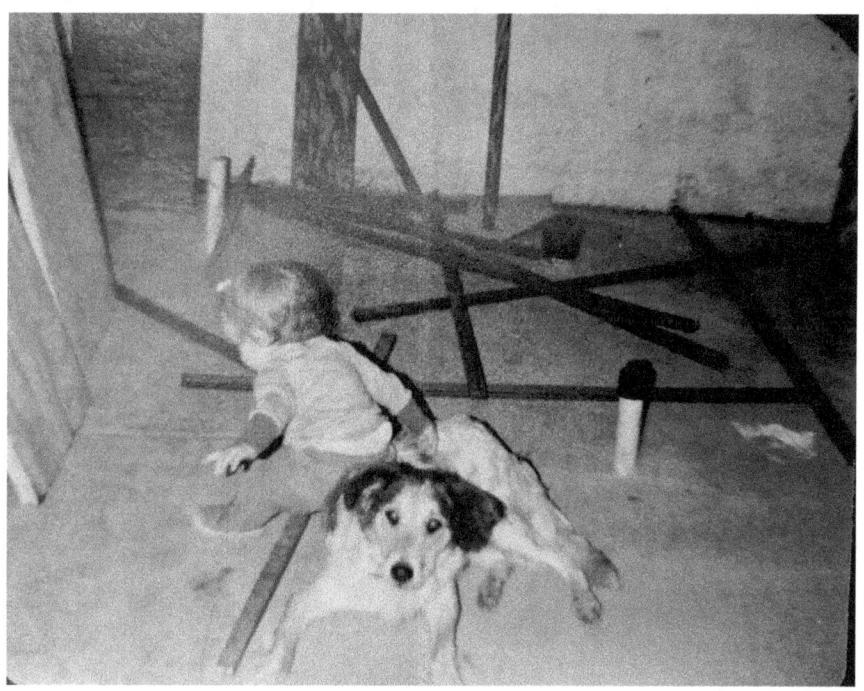

Baby Alena and Puppy Camille

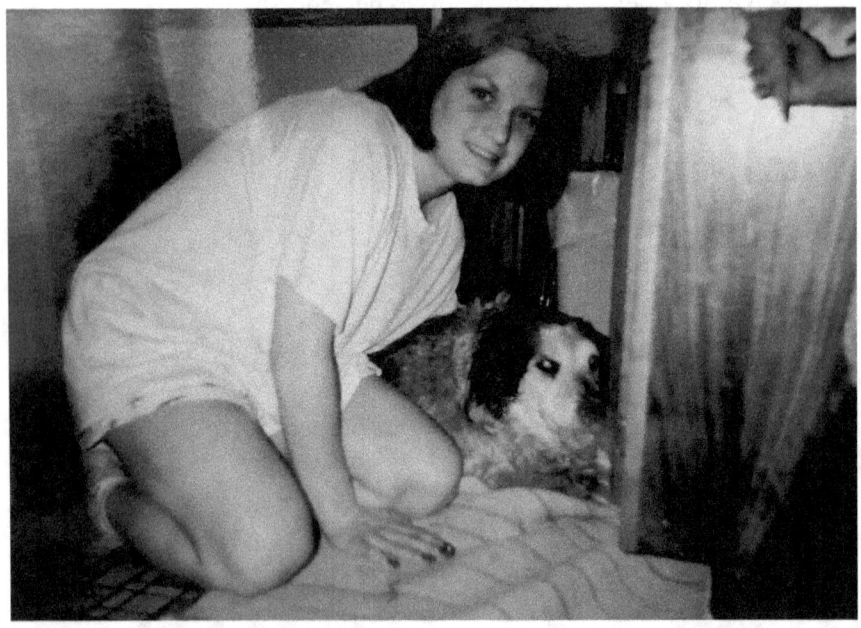

My last picture with Camille

Me and Salvatore

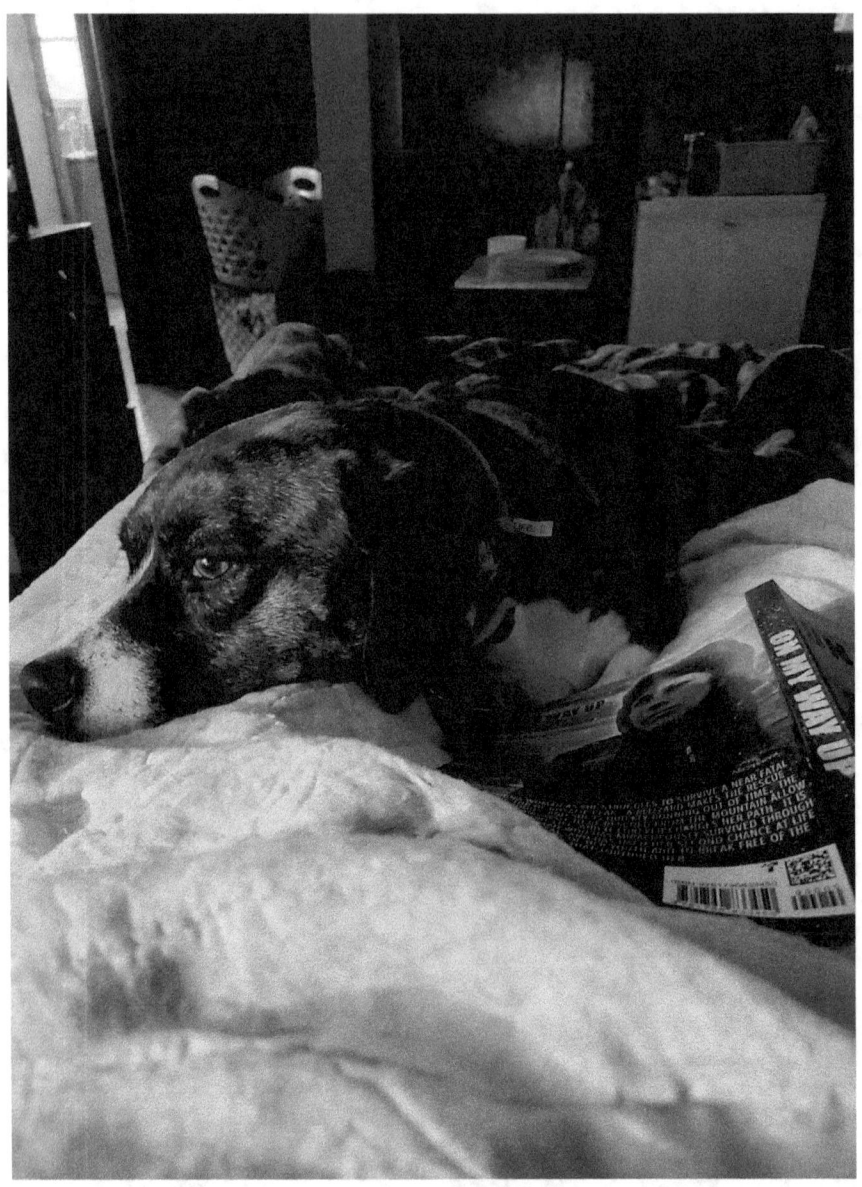

Salvatore doing what he does best: providing support as I nap and recover.

CHAPTER 12

FINAL THOUGHTS ON BEING BLESSED BY DEATH

Throughout my lifetime I've experienced many impactful deaths, as well as the Deaths of Self that allowed me to let go of beliefs that no longer serve me. I hope that as you read about my journey and the tools and practices I've developed along the way, you've found something that can help you on yours. Any journey, be it one of grief or other trials or tribulations, offers opportunities to learn lessons and expand our souls. Whether we get on board is up to us.

If you can't find the blessings or lessons yet, that is okay! Take your time and be gentle with yourself. Start with remembering your very favorite memories, start with loving yourself and others more deeply, start with forgiving yourself and others if necessary.

It is important to feel the feelings and allow them.

It's also okay to be okay after a death, even a tragic one. So many people have told me that guilt permeates any good feelings. I can relate, and I tell them what I tell myself: it is necessary to embrace all the beauty, joy, and laughter that life has to offer.

Do it in their honor.

Most importantly, remember that grief won't be linear. One day, or even one moment, I feel like I'm thriving and the next moment I feel paralyzed, like I can't make a decision, or simply, why bother? The difference is that I can feel that, allow that, and then shift out of it and back into who I want to be and who I need to be for myself and those I love.

So many people have told me how strong I am. And while I can acknowledge that, yes, I am very strong – physically, mentally, emotionally, and spiritually – it has taken effort to remain so. One of the greatest honors of my life is using my strength to be there for others so they can have that break from being the strong one. I strive for this in my personal life, as well as my professional one.

I try to breathe in each moment and accept it as it is. To look for the changes that need to be made or where I can be in flow and let go a little more. To look for the signs, symbols, and synchronicities from the Universe, my loved ones, angels, or deceased animal friends. My kids, my animals, my clients, nature, and most of all my loved ones in spirit, remind me of these lessons daily.

I continue to ask myself these questions.

What's my impact? What am I here for? What will my death mean to those I leave behind?

Will you join me in expanding your view of your life's meaning, your death of self needs, and what being blessed by death means to you?

TESTIMONIALS

"Working with Alena opened doors for me in my grief journey that I didn't know needed to be opened. I first contacted Alena after my husband died by suicide in 2020 to work through some blocks I was having in my grief process. I wasn't sure what I believed about past-life regression but was open to it if it would be helpful. My first session with Alena resulted in a successful past-life regression experience and began my journey to expand and deepen my spirituality. I was able to really look at my past grief to heal my present grief. I have learned so much from Alena and am grateful for her compassion and guidance."

~Alexandra

"As a mother of two children living with an incurable and progressive rare disease, I have had a difficult time accepting their diagnosis. My sessions with Alena have been transformative in helping me deal with the grief and anxiety surrounding their diagnosis. By aiding me in past-life regressions, she has helped give me the ability to be more present in this life. Our sessions have reiterated what I always thought to be true: that we are eternal souls having a human experience in order to learn, grow and evolve, which has brought me immense peace as I continue on the journey I am on with my children."

~Jillian

"On June 23, 2008, I woke up to my worst nightmare. My son was dead three days before his sixth birthday. I did CPR on him while we waited for the ambulance to arrive. I remember that day vividly. I carried it everywhere I went, the amount of feelings are unbelievable. The guilt, the anger all turn into self-hate. This was my fault. I should have done something different. To deal with all the emotions I started to cut. It is so much easier to deal with physical pain than all the emotional pain and guilt. Being in an abusive marriage didn't help. I got out of that relationship and started therapy, where I was taught to put my feelings and memories in a box and lock it away in my head; I was only to bring them out during therapy. That was helpful at the time but not long-term. I used alcohol as a crutch to deal with the pain. I also had a work addiction. I wanted to fill every moment of my day so I couldn't feel.

A few years ago I started on my own spiritual path away from religion. And in my journey, I met Alena. I absolutely loved her energy. So when she reached out to me about hypnosis therapy, I just had to try it. I was never one to think hypnosis therapy could help me. I was wrong. My first session was so powerful. I was able to see that horrible day from another perspective. I got to tell my past self that I did everything I could possibly have done. Not only did I get to see my son running to me with open arms, but also to hear his voice. He wasn't able to do this when he was alive. The weight that I carried for years was off my shoulders. The grief for him being gone will always be with me, but not the negative feelings that I carried for 15 years. I will always be grateful for what Alena has helped me achieve. I still have a lot of healing to do and look forward to all of my sessions with her."

~Rachele

ACKNOWLEDGMENTS

Matt, your support allowed this book to happen. Your belief in me has allowed me to believe in myself.

Issadora, my shining light in strength and unwavering belief, you've been my partner and helper at so many expos; without you this business could have never been. I will treasure all our adventures, especially the trips with just us and our magical time in Joshua Tree. IYKYK.

Jacob, you are the one who taught me to embrace my spiritual gifts and helped me to understand life and our souls on an even deeper level. I will be forever grateful.

Ian, you are one of my greatest teachers. You have taught me how to laugh more, play more, and be a little wild and crazy. Your thoughtfulness reminds me to do the same.

Bodhi, you weren't meant for this life, yet you completely changed the trajectory of mine. I know that your impact has been far-reaching and truly shows just how important one life can be, even when it was but a drop in the bucket.

To each of the people whose deaths I have written about, you changed my life for the better. I hope I have honored you in a way that you approve of.

There have been so many people who allowed this book to come together. It's going to be hard to list them all.

Lisa Sarick, you were the first author I knew personally and you inspired me to share my unique gifts with the world. You and Cindi's service for Bodhi meant so much.

Sunny Dawn Johnston, meeting you and Kris Voelker eleven years ago changed the trajectory of my life in the best ways possible. The person you are and the business you've created are a great inspiration.

Debi Appleton-Darr, your strength, belief in yourself, and your connection to Spirit are unparalleled. You have been my second-biggest cheerleader (behind Matt) and I wouldn't be who I am today without your guidance.

Arthur Keicher, I will be forever grateful for your mentorship. You have helped me to grow in my spiritual and metaphysical understanding, which has improved my life and the lives of my clients.

Alexandra Wyman, thank you for being you! We have had some epic adventures in the short time we've known each other. Presenting, traveling, and shooting for the stars together has been a highlight of my life. Without your encouragement and guidance this book wouldn't have come to fruition.

Sean B, thank you for running so many miles with me. Our talks about life and death and what it all means helped me write this book and explain my viewpoints more clearly.

Shawn F, thank you for expanding my experience with all that nature, Mother Earth, and all those who came before us have to offer.

I could go on forever. The names of the many amazing people who have crossed my path could fill another book. I live with gratitude in my heart for each of you.

And even to those who have shown what not to be, I am grateful.

ABOUT THE AUTHOR

A lena lives with Matt, her husband of twenty years, and their three living children, three dogs, and three cats in a small Western Pennsylvania town. She spends her free time reading, listening to podcasts, hiking, paddleboarding, playing games, and eating Matt's good cooking.

Alena is the proprietor of the mind, body, heart, and soul business Celebrate Every Step and hosts a podcast of the same name. She offers local or on-location individual sessions, classes, courses, expos, retreats, personal retreats and – her very favorite – sessions in nature as a Licensed Social Worker, a Clinical Hypnotherapist, Past Life Regressionist, psychic medium, and spiritual guide.

While each session is customized to the client's individual beliefs and needs, her overall focus is on mental, emotional, physical, and spiritual well-being. She helps people navigate trauma, suicidal ideation, self-harm, anxiety, a positive body and food relationship, a mind-body connection, awakening intuition and connecting to their Spirit Team, and especially navigating grief in all forms.

Some Fun Facts About Alena:

- She has a blue belt in Brazilian Jiu-jitsu – the first female in her gym to receive that distinction.
- She has a goal of hiking the entire 4,600 miles of the North Country Trail that runs from Vermont to South Dakota. She is slowly hiking the miles with her kids and dogs, approximately two to four miles at a time.
- The furthest distance she has covered at one time was a sixty-nine-mile race for her thirty-ninth birthday. It took her twenty hours and thirty-two minutes, which she ran in running sandals called "Paleoshoes," made by her uncle. A cousin and a friend joined her on the adventure, with her husband Matt serving as a roving aid station.
- Alena became a living donor in 2023 by donating a kidney to her dad.

How to Continue Your Healing Journey and Work With Alena

I am a lifelong learner, both from others I feel called to study and my own experiences, and am always incorporating this into the sessions I offer.

Individual sessions are customized to what the client and their soul need most. Some people say they don't know what they need; they just know they want things to be different from what they are. I am good at distilling down the presenting problem, and as we talk we always move into an understanding of what to work on. Once we enter hypnosis, the soul and subconscious will take us exactly where it most needs to go for the greatest healing.

We work on alleviating any physical, mental, or emotional pain, and we do any current or past life exploration that we need to. It helps to gain clarity and insight. It allows the client to do for themselves what they most need to do. That might be forgiveness of others or self, saying what they didn't get a chance to say at the time, soul-to-soul communication with those alive or deceased, and, most importantly, taking care of themselves in the ways they most needed but didn't get. Sometimes a soul hug of your younger self makes all the difference.

I work with people on everything from chakra clearing and balancing to intergenerational healing, inner child work, addressing past trauma, anxiety, depression, addictions, and so much more. In the simplest terms, I help clients let go of what no longer serves them so they can feel and function at their very best.

I also assist with these topics in a group class setting, during which I share what I'm learning on my spiritual journey. These are either scheduled by me or someone who brings together a group of friends or family or as a guest at retreats. A goal of mine has been to offer retreats. I was set to offer one in 2023 with Alexandra Wyman, but I postponed it to donate a kidney to my dad. The when, where, and with whom is still to be determined for a future retreat. After traveling to sacred sites in Glastonbury, Avebury and London, it would be a dream to bring others there on retreat to experience the divine healing it offered, so stay tuned.

I offer group hypnosis, mostly at seasonal changes. This helps with that energy shift and in engaging participants in a conscious conversation with me and their Spirit Team about the behaviors and beliefs they need to let go of. We then identify what they want to bring into their lives, how they truly want to be living. I weave that together for a beautiful group hypnosis that incorporates the energetic and astrological shifts in conjunction with those intentions and needs.

Connect with Alena

Learn more about Alena and her services, as well as more photos of the people, animals, and events mentioned in the book, at **celebrateeverystep.com**

Photo Gallery: **celebrateeverystep.com/bbd-gallery**

Find her podcast at **celebrateeverystep.com/category/podcast**

You can find more content and community interaction at **facebook.com/celebrateeverystep** and **instagram.com/celebrateeverystep**

Free guided meditation and hypnosis sessions at **youtube.com/user/alenakg**

Schedule a free discovery call and find upcoming sessions, classes, and courses at **celebrateeverystepscheduling.as.me**

BONUS GIFTS

Meditation to Meet a Loved One in Spirit

**celebrateeverystep.com/
bbd-bonus-meditation**

Spotify Playlist

celebrateeverystep.com/bbd-bonus-spotify